"I KILLED A MAN"

Xyrus

Dedication

To my Twin Flame,

In the darkest and most tumultuous chapters of my life, when the weight of pain, struggles and internal strife seemed insurmountable, you appeared as a beacon of light and hope. Your love, patience and presence have been a sanctuary of peace and strength, guiding me through the storm and helping me heal from the wounds I thought might never mend. You entered my life at the very pinnacle of my struggles, and with your boundless love, unwavering truth, and radiant positivity, you began to heal me in ways words cannot fully express. Thank you for everything that you are. And everything that you will become in this life. Success and prosperity follows you effortlessly and you are loved.

Your spirit is an endless source of inspiration. The depth of my love for you transcends this lifetime; you are my heartbeat, my muse, and the driving force behind every page of this book. It was your unwavering support and the sacred space you created for me that enabled me to find my voice and pen these words.

You are not just my love and my best friend; you are my greatest blessing. May our souls continue to find each other in every lifetime, and may the love we share remain eternal, boundless, and ever-growing. This book is but a small testament to the infinite gratitude and devotion I hold for you. Always and forever, you are my heart, my home

Acknowledgement

Writing this book has been an odyssey of profound reflection and overwhelming gratitude. Each word, each sentence, has been a step into the depths of my soul, unearthing memories, emotions, and lessons that have shaped the man I am today. It hasn't been an easy journey and it's far from over; at times, it felt like walking through fire, with every painful memory searing my heart, and every victory soothing the burns with the balm of resilience.

I owe much of my strength to the incredible people who stood by me during the darkest chapters of my life. They were the beacons of light in a world that often felt suffocating and hopeless, guiding me through the labyrinth of despair with unwavering faith and unrelenting love. These individuals were not just supporters; they were my pillars, holding me up when I felt too weak to stand, reminding me of the power within when I doubted my own worth. They were the voices that drowned out the noise of negativity and fear, whispering words of encouragement and strength when I needed them the most.

I think back to the times when I was on the brink of giving up, when the weight of injustice and pain seemed too heavy to bear. In those moments, it was the thought of those who believed in me, who saw the potential in me even when I couldn't, that kept me going. Their belief became my lifeline, pulling me out of the abyss and pushing me to fight harder, to rise above the circumstances that sought to break me.

Writing this book has been more than just telling my story; it has been an act of healing. It has allowed me to revisit the pain with a new perspective, to see it not as a source of weakness but as the crucible that forged my strength. Each chapter, each reflection, has been a reminder of the incredible journey I've been on—a journey that I could not have survived alone.

To those who stood by me, who fought for me, who never wavered in their support, this book is as much yours as it is mine. Your strength, your resilience, your unwavering belief in me have been the threads that held my story together. You are the heroes behind the scenes, the warriors who fought battles in the shadows so that I could find the light. My gratitude for you is boundless, and I hope that through these pages, you can see the impact you've had on my life.

As I write these final words, I am filled with a deep sense of peace and fulfillment. The journey hasn't been easy, but it has been worth every struggle, every tear, every sleepless night. This book is my testament to the power of resilience, the strength of the human spirit, and the unbreakable bonds of love and support. It is a tribute to the incredible people who believed in me, who never gave up on me, and who continue to inspire me every day. Without you, I would not be here. Thank you, from the bottom of my heart, for being my light in the darkest of times.

Shannon Fitzpatrick and Ron Bowden: Thank you so much for opening your home to me, for supporting, guiding, and caring for me as if I were your own. When I came home from jail, I was lost, but your patience and unwavering support helped me to find my way. Words cannot adequately express the love and admiration I have for you both.

Amy Kamp: You fought for a young man you knew nothing about. I'll never forget the day you visited me in jail to hear my plight. You weren't sure if I was innocent, but you gave me the time and opportunity to be heard. Your belief in me, even from that cell, is something I will cherish forever. Thank you for your compassion and dedication.

Shawn Jackson: First, I want to say I'm proud of your achievements and your transformation. You are a great man and an even better father. You went home, looked back, and took action to ensure I wasn't left behind. You fought for me tooth and nail, believed in me, and did everything in your power to support and encourage me. For that, I thank you, though words can't fully convey my gratitude.

Professor Matt Clair: Meeting you has been everything I hoped for and more. Thank you for seeing me, aiding me, and standing beside me. Your book sparked a desire in me to fight, live, and pursue a career in law. Your response to my letter brought a peace and comfort that few may ever know. Your kindness transcended those caged barriers and carried me forward.

To my Brothers by Loyalty: Edwin, Jey24k, Demun Mercer, Gizmo, Sahh, Mateo, Dom, Draco, Flex, Lj, Rob Salazar, DMoney, Smoke, Lil Joey, John Wolfe, Dion Warr, Travis, Tommy, Shaq G, Sjadi, Trey, Terrance, Lil Freddy, Davonte Miller, Anttione Benson, Myles Martin, Popstar, DJ Afo, DJ Quenezzzz, Angel Givens, Nacho Jamel J, Jitmann, H-Town Junior, JR, Murphy, Keno, Leo L, Lando, Supreme93, Jacorey Simon, Wildboijames, Lorne, Marzo, Murphy, Phet, Javonte Potter, Jamahl Johnson, Mims and anyone else who I may not have named here—thank you for answering those calls, staying by my side, and choosing me in my darkest hours. Thank you for helping me make my transition home.

Desto: Thank you for your love, your time, your heart, and your kindness. You are a star. I wish nothing but the best for you and your promising future.

To my family: Your love and support were not in vain. I cherish you all and will sacrifice my life to see you thrive and smile.

To my Mother: You are love, you are altruism at its greatest definition and that's all we know. Thank you for the love you give; only The Most High knows anything greater, that you have expressed to me far too well. The lessons learned from you shaped my heart and soul. And fortified my mind in a way that can never be defeated. My first and forever love. Your baby boy understands you, and I am beyond proud of your hard work and efforts. Know and believe that from the bottom of my heart. God bless our praying mothers and prosper their sons so that we can express the multitude of their unwavering love.

MANO AMIGA, my team: Thank you for welcoming me in, helping me get out, and supporting me relentlessly to this day. You embody true grit, passion, and servitude to others. Your work is grand, and your efforts are not unnoticed. MANO AMIGA is a movement not a label, and a marathon not a sprint, so keep pushing forward. The work that you all do is trying, however it is very necessary and I am beyond grateful that you are doing it. Made a grand difference in what my life could have been right now.

To **Murphy Ann Carter & TAVP: Thank you for not only believing in me as a person but also seeing the hope within my story. Murphy, I am deeply grateful for your unwavering presence, patience, and your willingness to go above and beyond for others, myself included. Your support has been nothing short of monumental, and your heartfelt advice means more to me than words can express.

To **Melinda Rothouse: When I first saw you in the jury box I was sure you thought I was guilty, I'm thankful for how wrong I was. You weren't condemning me, you were concerned for me. You were paying attention to every word you heard and it bothered you to your core so you did something about it. Thank you so much for doing something about it.

To **Karen Muñoz & Ricky T: I can't express enough gratitude for your unwavering dedication to fighting for my freedom. You are not just exceptional attorneys—you are true friends, allies, and an inspiration that fuels my own pursuit of a law degree. Your passion, empathy, and work ethic go far beyond the standard expectations of legal counsel, setting a powerful example for what justice should truly look like, both in Hays County and beyond. I just wish, Ricky T, that your chess game was as sharp as your legal skills!

To Pastor Darius Todd: Your unwavering love has been a beacon of divine grace in my life. From the moment we met, your simple yet profound question, "How can I help?" struck a chord deep within me. Since then, your steadfast support has been a transformative force, guiding me through spiritual, emotional, and physical challenges. I believe God is proud of your work, as am I. Your dedication to healing what was broken in me—and in many others—is a testament to your profound compassion. As you boldly declared, "We are bound together for life whether you like it or not," those words have become a cherished promise. Thank you for your unwavering support and the enduring impact you've made in my life.

To My Brother 4L, DeVonte J Amerson: Words often fall short of capturing the depth of what we share. What's understood between us doesn't require explanation. You reflect my heart and soul, echoing the unspoken bond we have. Your relentless dedication to provide and elevate the circumstances of those you love comes nothing short of mine and the essence of The most High within us. Our minds alone are unstoppable and together we remain untouchable. You can do no wrong in my eyes brother and you never have.

To **Dila Rosemond: I love you brother, and I pray that you are well, you will forever have me in your corner.

To **Paul Parash:**

Though our differences are undeniable, I want you to know that I am forever grateful for the efforts you made to set me free. I sincerely pray that you are blessed, that your life is filled with the rewards you seek, and that your time with me was not in vain. I hope you can reconnect with the passion and purpose that first led you to this path—the true essence of what it means to zealously represent someone who desperately needs your voice.

The odds are often against you, yes, but even more so, the world is against the defendant. In those moments, you are their only defense, their only hope. Take pride and honor in the level of service you provide because, in those dark and lonely moments, you are the light that can guide someone to a chance at life again.

To **Bobby Joe Harper: The fight's not over. We shared the same prosecutor, though our fates were different. Know that you are not alone and will not be left behind. You are innocent and you have been terribly wronged. But you are strong and you will prevail. We love and support you, and will continue to do so through this journey.

This is my village, near and far—my hope and my reason.

In life, we accumulate layers of experiences, traumas, and learned behaviors. "Killing a man" is the act of peeling back these layers, exposing the core of who we are. Each "man" represents a version of ourselves that has been shaped by hardship, failure, or societal expectations. To reach our true potential, we must strip away these personas, one by one, until only the authentic self remains. It's a gradual shedding of what is no longer needed to make space for personal growth and healing.

Contents

Introduction

On March 5, 2018, at exactly 3:45 PM, my life took a sharp, nightmarish turn that I could never have anticipated. The day had started like any other, with me diligently setting up a treatment table at my job as a Physical Therapy Technician. I was focused, methodically preparing for the next patient, completely unaware that within moments, my entire world would be upended. As I arranged the equipment, the door suddenly burst open, and the room was instantly flooded with an overwhelming and menacing presence—several heavily armed officers in full military gear, their assault rifles aimed directly at me. The sight was surreal, like something out of a movie, but this was no fiction. The San Marcos Police Department (SMPD) detectives and Task Force had arrived, and their target was me.

"Cyrus Gray, don't move!" one of them commanded, his voice slicing through the air with an authority that left no room for resistance. My heart pounded in my chest, my mind racing to catch up with the reality unfolding before me. I was paralyzed with shock, unable to fully comprehend what was happening. The room, once a place of healing and care, had transformed into a battlefield, and I was caught in the crossfire. The officers moved quickly and efficiently, cuffing my hands with a force that made it clear this was no mistake. As they led me out of the building, I could feel the weight of their accusations pressing down on me, heavier than the metal around my wrists.

My coworkers and patients stood frozen in disbelief, their faces a mixture of confusion, fear, and shock. The air was thick with tension, the silence deafening as they watched me, the person they had worked alongside and trusted, being dragged away like a dangerous criminal. The disbelief in their eyes mirrored my own internal turmoil—how could this be happening? I had done nothing to deserve this, yet here I was, my life unraveling in front of everyone I knew. The humiliation of being publicly arrested was overwhelming, but even worse was the gnawing fear of the unknown. What awaited me beyond those doors?

Outside, I was handed over to Detectives Sandra Spriegel and Dave Campbell, who were waiting in an unremarkable soccer mom minivan, its bland appearance belying the intensity of what was unfolding. The Task Force that had stormed into my life with such force vanished as quickly as they had appeared, leaving me alone with the detectives. Lead Detective Sandra Spriegel wasted no time in declaring my fate: I was under arrest for a capital murder that had occurred in 2015 in San Marcos, Texas. Her voice was cold, mechanical, as if she were reading from a script. She demanded to know the whereabouts of a close friend of mine, her eyes probing for any sign of weakness. But I knew better than to fall into her trap. I chose silence, understanding that anything I said could and would be twisted against me. "I need a lawyer," I stated firmly, my voice steady despite the turmoil raging inside me. Her eyes pierced my like daggers.

The detectives shot off without another word, their minivan tearing through the streets of Houston like a high-powered sports car. As we sped away, the city around me became a blur—a dizzying whirl of lights and shadows that seemed to stretch and twist, melting into a surreal nightmare. I was being pulled from the life I knew, and every passing second plunged me deeper into the unknown. Moments later, we exited the highway, and Detective Dave Campbell glanced back at me, good cop- bad cop I guess. "Hey man, it's just you and us now," he said. "This is your last chance to tell us what you know and help yourself—off the record, of course."

I could feel my pulse pounding in my ears. "Do you see how y'all just came for me? Bro, you could've called my phone. You're not here to help me. I need a lawyer," I replied, my voice steady but my mind reeling. The vehicle jolted, each bump in the road sending fresh waves of fear and disbelief crashing over me. Finally, we pulled into a gas station in Sealy, Texas, the van idling under the harsh fluorescent lights. The weight of the situation bore down on me, intensifying with every second that passed, as I sat there, trapped between fate and fear.

We waited there for an SMPD patrol car to transport me the rest of the way to San Marcos. The ride that followed was grueling; I sat cuffed in the backseat, the cold metal biting into my wrists as my mind raced with a thousand questions, none of which had comforting answers. I stared out at the dark, unfamiliar roads, knowing that each mile was taking me further from any semblance of normalcy. I was kidnapped if you ask me.

Late that night, we finally arrived in San Marcos. The officers made a pit stop at Popeyes for food, a bizarre and surreal detour given the gravity of the situation. They even dropped one officer off at his home, leaving me shackled in the backseat, a prisoner in every sense of the word. The mundanity of their actions only heightened the absurdity of my situation—here they were, grabbing dinner and going about their lives, while mine was being systematically dismantled. But when it came to policing and justice I would come to find that everything was odd in this small town

Finally, I was taken to the police department, where I waited another agonizing thirty minutes before being transferred to Hays County Jail. Thrown into a filthy holding cell, I was surrounded by other detainees, freezing on piss-soaked concrete that reeked of despair and neglect. The reality of my situation began to settle in, the cold seeping into my bones as I made my first call—to my girlfriend at the time, who was already with my mother. I could hear the worry in her voice, a reflection of the chaos that had already started to ripple through the lives of my loved ones. The detectives had begun their relentless "HUNT" as they called it, terrorizing my family and friends in their sick attempt to pin the murder on me and my childhood friend.

The next day, I was magistrated and informed of my charges. The weight of the words "capital murder" hung in the air like a death sentence. Lead Detective Sandra Spriegel, with her unwavering gaze, recommended no bond, sealing our fate. We were trapped.

As you read this introduction, I invite you to consider how I found myself in such a harrowing situation. How does an ordinary day at work transform into a life-altering nightmare? What led me to become the target of a heavily armed task force, wrongly accused of a crime I had no part in? In those moments, as my world unraveled, it wasn't just my freedom that was being taken—it was my identity, my peace of mind, and the trust of those around me. How did it come to this, and why was I the one standing on the other side of those rifles? These are the questions I grappled with as I sat, cuffed and silenced, my fate seemingly sealed by forces beyond my control.

The journey leading up to that moment didn't start with flashing lights or handcuffs—it began long before, shaped by a series of events that I couldn't have foreseen. As you turn the page, I ask you to step into my shoes and reflect on how a life so carefully built can be torn apart in an instant. What decisions, what relationships, what twists of fate contributed to my being in that room on March 5, 2018? The answers to those questions lie in the chapters ahead, starting with the very first step that set me on a path I never intended to walk.

"The truth will set you free, but first it will piss you off." — **Gloria Steinem**

Chapter I:

New Beginnings

I was born in the vibrant and culturally rich land of West Africa. My family and I lived in a blue clay house in Monrovia, Liberia with several other relatives. My early childhood was a tapestry woven with the warmth of family, the resilience of a close-knit community, and the traditions that connected us to our roots. Our family hailed from Liberia, Ghana, Guinea, Gambia, Cote D'ivoire and the surrounding countries, and we lived together in that humble blue clay house that was always alive with the sounds of laughter, conversations, and the daily hustle of life. That's what I remember at least.

In those early years, the bonds of family were everything. I remember the endless procession of relatives who flowed in and out of our home, each bringing their own stories, struggles, and joys. A web of connection that shaped my understanding of the world.

I remember the laughter and chaos of playing with my cousins, the way we would spend hours outside, letting our imaginations run wild. My older cousin had this strange habit of pulling his eyelids back to scare us—honestly, it was downright unsettling, and we'd take off running, shrieking with a mix of fear and laughter. Just when we thought we'd escaped his bizarre antics, he'd completely change the mood, doing impressive backflips or walking on his hands, instantly captivating us all over again. Our fear would quickly melt away, replaced by wide-eyed amazement and excitement. We couldn't help but be drawn back to him, mesmerized by his acrobatics, and before long, we were eagerly trailing behind him, chasing the next thrill he had in store. He had this magnetic energy that made even the scariest moments unforgettable.

Our house was a sanctuary where everyone was welcome, no matter how long they stayed or how little they had. It was a place where my mother and aunts, women of extraordinary strength, would walk long distances from time to time to fetch water, carrying the weight of their families on their shoulders with a quiet determination that spoke volumes about their character. I still remember the time my cousin Papoose almost pushed me off a bridge walking with them. And walking down the aisle as a ring bearer for my aunt's wedding. When I was a baby I wouldn't eat for some reason and I can still recall very vividly these women having to hold me down and force feed me. A scary but necessary act for a difficult child. These women were my first examples of resilience and love. Their unwavering dedication to their loved ones left an indelible mark on my heart.

"Family is not an important thing, it's everything." – **Michael J. Fox**

Even as a young child, I was a thinker, constantly contemplating the world around me and my place within it. My mind was always buzzing with questions, and my heart was filled with a deep love for my family and those close to me. These early experiences shaped my identity and laid the groundwork for the person I would become. But life, as it often does, had other plans for me.

At a very young age, my life took a dramatic turn when my family decided to leave Africa and move to America. Our childhood was one of joy, bonds and laughter but, our homelands were at constant war, so inevitably, when the time was right my parents made the decision to relocate. But they couldn't take everybody. And at first they couldn't take anybody. Once they were settled they made way for my older brother and I to join them.

My older brother and I, mere children at the time, embarked on a journey that would change our lives forever. We boarded a plane, flying alone across vast oceans, to reunite with our parents in a land that was completely foreign to us. The flight was long, and as we soared through the skies, I couldn't help but wonder what awaited us on the other side. I remember being chased around the airport because I wasn't willing to take the vaccinations to be accepted into the country. All I saw was several needles and I wasn't having it, not one bit.

When we finally arrived in America, we were met by a driver who took us to our new home, where our parents were waiting. The reunion was bittersweet; while the joy of being together again was overwhelming, it was tinged with the pain of leaving behind our oldest sister and many of our cousins. This separation was a stark reminder of the sacrifices my mother and father had made for us, a burden that weighed heavily on my young heart. We were refugees in the windy city and the cold was sharper than glass.

Chicago was a world away from the warmth and familiarity of Africa. We found ourselves living in a trailer home with my grandmother, aunts, and cousins on my father's side. The cold, windy streets of Chicago were a harsh contrast to the sun-soaked days of my childhood. The transition was disorienting, and I often longed for the sense of belonging that had defined my early years.

It was during this time that my little sister was born, and she quickly became the light of my life. She was my first true love outside of my mother, and her presence brought a new sense of purpose and joy to our lives. However, even as I cherished this new addition to our family, the intense sibling rivalry between my older brother and me continued to simmer.

Our fights were epic, often resembling the action-packed scenes from a movie in kid form, but they were more than just childhood squabbles—they were our way of coping with the constant changes and challenges we faced.

The cultural shock of moving to America was profound. The humor, the customs, and the way people interacted were all so different from what we had known in Africa, even people of our own skin color. The American sense of humor, in particular, was perplexing to me at the time. It often seemed rooted in pain, in the belittlement of others, something I struggled to understand. There was a distinct lack of the communal spirit that had been the cornerstone of our lives in Africa. In our new environment, it felt as though everyone was more focused on highlighting others' flaws in an attempt to mask their own insecurities. The sense of community, of belonging to a village, was missing, and it left a void in my heart.

After several years in the harsh cold of Chicago, Illinois we made another move—this time to Houston, Texas. I braced myself for yet another cultural shock, half-expecting to find myself learning how to ride a horse, given the stereotypes I had heard about Texas. But instead of cowboys and horses, I was confronted with a different challenge: the sweltering heat. It was hotter than anything I had ever experienced, even in Africa. We moved around the city of Houston a lot in those years, trying to find our place to come home and dealing with the struggles of immigrants trying to make a living for their family in a foreign place. Despite the challenges, these experiences in Chicago and Houston were crucial in shaping my understanding of the world and my place in it.

In Houston, our lives continued to be marked by instability. We moved frequently, sometimes year after year, and our financial situation was precarious at best. We lived in poverty, but my mother and father did everything in their power to shield us from its harshest realities. My mother worked multiple jobs, tirelessly juggling her responsibilities to ensure that we had a roof over our heads and food on the table. Her strength and selflessness were the foundation of our endurance.

My father was a part of our lives too, but that's a story for another time. I love my father and understand him now more than I ever did. In those days, more often than not, the responsibility of looking after my younger sister and me fell squarely on my older brother's shoulders while our mother was at work, and our father was out hustling however he could or at "work."

I can still vividly recall those days when the three of us would be home alone, my brother and I scrambling to prepare bottles for my baby sister. Anytime someone knocked on the door, we'd kill the lights and TV, sitting in silence, holding our breath as if that would make it clear that noone was home. Then there were the times when we'd join other kids to sneak into abandoned apartments, daring each other to put forks in running microwaves, just to see what would happen. Spoiler alert—nothing good ever came from that. One careless day, we caused our sister to end up in the emergency room. We had been arguing while trying to heat her food, and in the chaos, placed a jar of boiling water right within her reach. In an instant, she knocked it over, scalding her leg with blistering burns that still haunt me. That wasn't a good phone call to mom at all.

Another time, we convinced ourselves to break into the pool, despite me not knowing how to swim. My brother, always the risk-taker at that time, easily persuaded me to jump in with him. Without hesitation, I leaped into the deep end, and within seconds, panic set in. I realized I was drowning, thrashing wildly in the water, dragging him down with me as he tried to save us both. It was pure chaos; he was struggling to keep us afloat, and I was too scared to stop flailing. That moment was the second time I almost died. My brother wasn't much of a talker back then, and even though I didn't fully grasp it at the time, I now understand the weight of the burden he carried.

He had been forced to grow up far too quickly, shouldering the responsibility of caring for us while never getting the chance to fully enjoy his own childhood. He was my protector, my caretaker, my guardian—roles he took on without question, sacrificing his freedom so that we could have ours.

But that didn't mean our fights stopped. On the contrary, they intensified. When my favorite cousin moved in with us, the dynamic shifted once more. It became two older, broken Mastiffs against a broken red-nosed pit, and our battles were as fierce as ever. But, these chaotic, tumultuous times never severed the love we had for one another to this day, each forged in the fire of our shared experiences.

My mother was the glue that held us together. She was a mother to everyone, no matter how they came into our lives. Throughout my youth, our home was a refuge for cousins, aunts, uncles, and friends who needed a place to heal and grow. Despite having so little, there was never a moment when my mother wouldn't make it enough for everyone. She extended her love and care not just to those under our roof, but also to those back in Africa, ensuring that her family, near and far, was taken care of. Especially her favorite child—me.

One memory stands out vividly from those years. I'll never forget the day my mother came home to find me in tears because my older cousin and brother wouldn't let me play the PS2 with them. Without a moment's hesitation, she put me in the car and took me to buy a GameCube Nintendo with one controller and three games, even though we couldn't afford it. Her relentless love knew no bounds, and in that moment, she showed me that she would always be there for me, no matter what.

When my favorite uncle, Uncle G, moved in with us, I finally had someone I could truly connect with. He was more than just family; he was my ally, my escape. We spent countless summer nights sitting outside under the stars, listening to music as he freestyled effortlessly, the words flowing out of him like water. He'd puff on Black n' Milds back-to-back, filling the air with that distinct, sweet scent that clung to the night. Uncle G had this infectious energy, always smiling and joking, yet beneath that happiness lay one of the saddest life stories I had ever heard. He was one of my father's many siblings—most of whom my dad never even knew. Some of them he still hasn't met to this day. You see, my Grandfather Cyrus was what you'd call a rolling stone, drifting from place to place, leaving behind children who never really knew him. I never met my grandfather, and as for my mother's father, he was just as much a ghost in my life. But my mom never fails to remind me how much I look like him, a piece of a puzzle I've never fully seen. The only Grandparent of mine that I actually know is my fathers mother. I only have stories of the others.

Uncle G, on the other hand, was a living, breathing connection to that untold family story. He grew up on the East Coast, bouncing in and out of jail for reasons I didn't care to ask about. To me, he wasn't his past; he was just my Uncle G, the man with long dreadlocks that fell all the way down to his waist, the man who would go to the ends of the earth to make me laugh. His presence was like a breath of fresh air in an otherwise heavy household. He never judged, never complained, and always made sure that everyone felt seen. I don't know where he is today—our paths have drifted apart—but I hope he's still out there somewhere, alive and well, maybe still freestyling under the stars like we used to. Wherever he is, I'll always hold on to the warmth and light he brought into my life, and I hope he's found peace on his own.

These early years, marked by upheaval and adaptation, laid the foundation for my resilience. They taught me the importance of family, the strength to endure, and the ability to navigate and thrive in different cultures. This chapter of my life, filled with love, struggle, and growth, set the stage for the person I would become.

Chapter II:

HOUSTON

The Movie's gonna be crazy...

The metaphor of "killing a man" represents the painful yet necessary process of personal evolution. Each "man" symbolizes outdated or harmful versions of the self, holding back growth. To evolve into the person we are destined to be, we must shed these old layers—confronting, dismantling, and ultimately eradicating the pieces of ourselves that no longer serve us. It is not an act of violence but a conscious decision to let go, embracing transformation and allowing new, healthier identities to emerge.

Chapter III:

Life Behind Bars

"Out of suffering have emerged the strongest souls; the most massive characters are seared with scars."

— **Khalil Gibran**

Part I: Life Behind Bars

Once I realized I was officially booked into Hays County Jail. I noticed my childhood friend DeVonte had also been arrested and booked. The first words to me from a correctional officer were:

"Get comfortable; you're gonna be here awhile."

Little did I know how true those words would be.

DeVonte and I were separated—he was placed in dorm D2-8, a 24-man tank, while I was sent to dorm D1-3, a 16-man max tank. My new reality was a cramped, hostile space filled with Mexicans, racist whites, and only two other Black men. The conditions were inhumane: three worn-down tables, a single barely functional phone, and a lone TV mounted so close above it that it seemed to press against our thoughts. The so-called amenities were just as dismal—two metal showers, two toilets, and a sink all crammed mere feet from where we ate. At night, we were locked in eight-man cages, completely cut off from the dayroom, water, or the phone.

Jail sucked to say the least. The majority of the guards took pleasure in punishing and humiliating us—or at least, that's how it felt. They stripped us of our dignity with every calculated act of cruelty. Those who dared show even a flicker of humanity were ridiculed and reprimanded by their peers. Fear and aggression ruled over both inmates and correctional officers alike, creating an unspoken law that compassion was weakness. Each day felt like a battle—not just for physical survival, but for the preservation of my mind, my identity, my very humanity. I clung to hope, desperate to escape the endless cycle of suffering and reclaim the life that had been stolen from me.

There were countless moments behind those walls where life and death balanced on a knife's edge. Moments of intentional dehumanization. Moments when our so-called "protectors" chose to ignore suffering—or worse, encouraged it. One of the most haunting memories came in my last years of incarceration, on the "New" side of the jail, in dorm F1, cell 21. It was there that my young friend Jit, a kid with severe asthma, almost died because of the guards' and medical staff's blatant negligence.

Jit, like many others, had been denied something as basic as an inhaler, a necessity for his survival. Without it, the suffocating nights in that place became a silent predator, tightening its grip around his lungs. I still hear the ragged sound of his wheezing, the way his body trembled as he fought for each breath. I first noticed his struggles when he became my cellmate, but that night was different—he was losing the battle.

He collapsed, gasping for air, while I repeatedly pressed the call button, my heart pounding in my chest. But as always, the guards ignored it.

My frustration erupted into desperation. I pounded on the cell door until my knuckles bled, refusing to be another silent witness to their cruelty. When the guards finally arrived, they didn't come to help. They came in numbers, barking orders, demanding Jit to state his name. But he couldn't speak. He couldn't even breathe. Watching them stand there, unmoved by his suffering, something inside me snapped. I unleashed a storm of words that cut deeper than any punch I was ready to throw. Only then—only when they saw the fire in my eyes, the unrelenting rage in my stance—did they finally call for medical assistance.

They punished us for it, of course. Locked us down for "disobeying direct orders." But I didn't care. Jit was alive.

I'd do it all over again in a heartbeat.

I love that kid like a brother. And I pray every day that he's out there somewhere, thriving—far from the darkness we endured together.

D1-3: The Beginning of the Nightmare

My first day in D1-3, I walked into the tank noticeably angry, with tunnel vision. Inmates of other races looked at me crazy but didn't say a word. One of the only other Black men in the dorm approached me after I placed my belongings on my bunk. He introduced himself, but his body told a story before he even spoke—three broken ribs, a dislocated knee, and a shoulder out of place, all injuries from his arrest and pretrial detention. He had been incarcerated for months without receiving any medical treatment. I popped his shoulder back into place and showed him ways to alleviate the pain in his knee. There was nothing I could do for his ribs.

During my first week, an elderly man attempted to hang himself while we slept. Inmates had to hold him up while others banged on the glass windows and rattled the caged gates to get the guards' attention. They ignored us. I had witnessed suicide attempts before, but this was different. In past experiences, the individuals hesitated or sought help in their actions. This old man hung there smiling before we reached him.

The Battle for Medical Attention

From the beginning, I suffered unbearable pain from my wisdom teeth. Before my arrest, I had a dental appointment scheduled to have them removed. In those first weeks of incarceration, I submitted countless medical requests and spoke to several correctional officers daily, begging for help. My pleas were ignored.

One day, during regular med rounds, I went to the sallyport—a small, claustrophobic room between two dorms and the hallway—to demand answers. Before even checking my file, the nurse carelessly said, "The dentist came yesterday, and you refused to see them." I blacked out. When I came to, I had several taser beams on my chest and face, and the echoes of guards shouting for me to get on the ground brought me fully back to consciousness. As soon as I took one knee, they pounced, all of them at once. At least I wasn't tased—yet.

They forcibly escorted me in cuffs, surrounded by guards. As I was dragged out, I saw other inmates pressed against their windows, shouting and banging in response to the spectacle. I was moved to D2-8, a 24-man dorm. But my time there was short-lived.

Brief Reunion, Sudden Separation

Being in D2-8 was initially a relief. It was more spacious, less restrictive, and housed a majority of the Black inmates—including my co-defendant and brother, DeVonte. The moment we saw each other, we embraced, as if it had already been half a decade. But my relief was fleeting. The guards immediately realized we were co-defendants and separated us within minutes. Over the years, I would come to learn that DeVonte and I were the only co-defendants they actively kept apart. We were also ordered to remain off the transfer list, ensuring that our pretrial incarceration remained indefinite. It all made sense—there was never a case against us. The State of Texas, San Marcos Police Department, former Texas Ranger Jimmy Schroeder, and Hays County Sheriff's Office had arrested us with no real evidence, hoping to build a case from our despair.

Within a week, I was forcibly moved back to D1-3. Apparently, some inmates had rioted for my return. I had no idea *WTF* they would do that..

A Night of Chaos: The Riot

Months into my detention, I was falsely accused of inciting a major riot, landing me in administrative segregation for 60 days. That night was something out of a Call of Duty scene. I awoke to the chaotic screams of guards armed with guns and tasers, their voices drowned by the clamor of inmates who had reached their breaking point. Makeshift masks covered their faces, and our rough mats—our only bedding— became shields against the relentless onslaught of mace and tasers. The floor was slick with fluids used as a crude defense. Every fist clenched was ready to face new charges, all in a desperate attempt to be heard.

Corporal Ontiveros had sparked the chaos. He had a twisted ritual on "CHAIN" nights, the evenings when inmates were transferred. He would tour the dorms, mocking inmates about whether they were on the list. This time, it backfired. Some inmates had trials or meetings with their attorneys the next morning and refused to be transferred. They weren't going for it. I wasn't on the list, so I followed my routine and went to sleep. I woke up to madness.

The riot ended with everyone tased, maced, and repeatedly slammed on their heads while cuffed—seemingly for the guards' amusement.

The Death of Manny

Among those with me that night was a young man named Manny. A tender soul, he had been sitting in jail for months over a theft charge, a minor crime in the grand scheme of our suffering. He had dreams of becoming a rapper and often shared freestyles that lightened our spirits.

Weeks after the riot, Manny died of a brain aneurysm while in custody. His sudden death shook us to our core. He was only 20 years old. No one was held accountable. His absence became a haunting reminder of how easily lives were discarded in that place. A young man full of potential, erased as if he had never existed.

The Revolving Door of Transfers

By the time I was released on bond, I had cycled through nearly every male dorm in that jail. I moved from D1-3 to D2-

8, then D2-7, back to D1-3, then to administrative segregation, D1-2, D1-4, A1, to F1 when the new section of the jail opened, then F4, back to F1, F3, and finally walked free of chains from D1-4.

My name became notorious—guards despised me, and among inmates, I was either respected or reviled. But regardless of how I was perceived, I wasn't going for No Monkey Business. I kept my mind focused on getting home. I reminded myself every day that this was not my world, and it would not define the rest of my life.

Administrative SEG: Isolation

The Isolation of Administrative Segregation was torturous. I had no phone, commissary, or visitation privileges—just a small cell with white walls, a bunk, a toilet and shower. And I had just run out of all my food. I was COOKED.

I sat in that cold small SEG cell for three days before I was brought any of my property. Or seen by medical staff or even spoken to about what would happen next. I slept on a cold small metal bunk with no mat or blanket in my torn up t-shirt and pants. I had no socks because they were stripped off after our repeated body slamming to be searched for weapons and or contriband of any kind. When a guard finally came to see me, it was Ontiveros. He presented me with a right up and said, "you're being written up for inciting a riot, you can take a punishment of 30 days in SEG now or go to a trial for the write up to try to argue its dismissal". I chose to take it to trial, because I was not involved until I absolutely had to be. For my own safety, and more so I refused to be blamed for anything and risk looking worse when I have to go to actual court or trial for a Capital Murder Case.

At the hearing for my write up I was taken to a small office in shackles where other ranking officers were waiting. Ontiveros was present. They told me I was being written up for inciting a riot and that my punishment would be 30 days in seg. Then asked, "how do you plea?" I said firmly, "Not guilty". I had no part in inciting a riot as charged. I was just the only person from that night that wasn't sent on "CHAIN". I then informed them that I woke up to a riot. I asked to see the video footage of that night to prove that I had no involvement and it showed just that. Me in my bunk asleep with a towel wrapped around my eyes to protect my eyes from the never dimming jail lights. "Look, that's me right there, you can clearly see I'm sleeping. And I don't wake up until yall bust the cages open screaming with tasers and mace!" I advocated. They were unmoved.

"Well you're very influential Gray, if you tell those guys to do something they'll do it so if you ask us we believe you were the mastermind of it all." a Corporal followed. I didn't give in.

"Hell nahh, that's some bullshit. You can clearly see I had nothing to do with this shit from the video!!"

I shouted, pointing with my two shackled hands. "I'm not finna take no punishment for something I didn't do. And besides, none of that would have even happened if your corporal didn't go around telling people they are gonna be on CHAIN and shit. Isn't that a security breach in the first place? You should be getting on his ass about all this but, clearly, yall are always gonna lie, cheat and steal for your own right. You got me ********************"...

You get the point.

They took me out of the room for a moment to talk about it. When I was brought back they informed me that 30 days segregation had now turned into a punishment of 30 days of Administrative Segregation. And that I could appeal their decision if I wanted, megalomaniacs. Their sick tone was evidence of much of a waste of effort that appeal would be. However I didn't care. I wasn't worried about petty powertrips, my mind was focused on my pending Capital Murder Charge and a paper trial to build my defense at any cost, this appeal was a part of that cost. I was taken back to my Seg cell. In cuffs and ankle shackles. When I got there I was demanded to face the wall and put one leg up at a time for the ankle shackles to be removed. The guard then demanded I remain facing the wall until he exited the cell, backing out with his hand on his taser and his eyes on me. Once he was outside safely he slammed the door and opened the small window on it– it was no bigger than the size of this book– he then ordered me to turn around and walk to the door. I had to stick my arms out of the small food slot so he could remove the wrist cuffs that squeezed life out of my hands. And then he was gone. The room was silent.

Moments later Corporal Ontiveros came with my property in shambles. He opened the door and threw the bag containing all of my belongings on the floor. "Let me talk to you Gray", he said cynically. "I know you're thinking about writing that appeal but, I'll tell you what. If you leave it alone I might be able to work out shortening your Seg time," he concluded. I was baffled to think that this type of behavior actually worked on people, but it made sense why it would. You stripe away everything from a person including their self worth and dignity, it can become very easy to have your way with them.

I declined and demanded a grievance form as well. He wasn't happy about it. And brazenly informed me that if I followed through he would be sure to MAX me out by increasing my punishment to 60 days of administrative seg. And he held true to the threats. 60 Days of Administrative Segregation, no phone privileges, visitation privileges, or commissary privileges.

Studies show that conditions like these for more than 15 days are considered torture. I was fed through a small slot in the door, and the portions were so meager that survival depended on outside support for commissary purchases.Studies have shown a strong connection between segregation or solitary confinement in jail and prison and the experience of torture-like conditions. Solitary confinement often involves isolating individuals for 22 to 24 hours a day in small, windowless cells with minimal human contact, which can have severe psychological and physical consequences.

Research indicates that prolonged segregation can lead to symptoms consistent with torture. These include severe anxiety, depression, hallucinations, paranoia, and even symptoms of post-traumatic stress disorder (PTSD). The World Health Organization and the United Nations consider prolonged solitary confinement (beyond 15 days) to be a form of torture due to its harmful effects on mental health.

A study published in *Science Advances* in 2019 showed that even short periods of solitary confinement can lead to deteriorated mental health, and the effects can last well beyond the period of isolation. Additionally, the United Nations' "Mandela Rules" explicitly outline that solitary confinement should not exceed 15 consecutive days, as longer periods are likely to cause irreversible psychological harm.

There is also evidence that solitary confinement exacerbates pre-existing mental health issues, making it particularly harmful for individuals with conditions like schizophrenia or bipolar disorder. A report by the National Institute of Justice highlighted that people with mental health disorders are often placed in solitary confinement more frequently, intensifying their symptoms and making recovery challenging.

In sum, the relationship between segregation and torture in prison settings is well-documented, with solitary confinement linked to severe psychological harm, which in turn has been recognized by many international organizations as a form of torture or cruel, inhuman, and degrading treatment.

In those 60 days, I came close to losing my sanity like many others around me that I could hear, but could not see. To combat the isolation, I turned to exercise, reading and creativity. I wrote movies, created a cartoon series, and devised business plans. I sought solace in my faith and read books to fortify my mind. My loved ones' thoughtful letters, doodles, and pictures were a lifeline, constantly reminding me that I had to keep going, that I would eventually go home. I was only taken out of the cell for one hour of rec. Once or a week, if they remembered. Rec was just another small cell size tank at the end of the hallway. This cell was no different from the one I now lived in with the exception of having a broken basketball hoop and a chain link roof that allowed visibility of the sun, moon and rain.

My Seg was extremely cold and the walls around it were so thin you could hear all of the pain and misery of the suffering people around you. There are a few things I'll never forget about jail. That time in Administrative Seg. was one of them. I remember one day I was in my cell drawing portraits of my niece and nephew, and a guard came to the window to inform and mock me all at the same time. "Rec day Gray looks like Jesus is mad at you today it's raining like crazy out there, I don't know if I can take you," he finished.

"Shiiid I'ma make Jesus smile today," I responded, not caring if it was a Hurricane raining hail and fire outside. I needed to see the sky. When I got to the Rec. yard it was raining. I didn't care. I did my usual "outside" workout that I would do on Rec. days and shot the basketball around for a while after. In the middle of my workout, I noticed the rain was going away, then it stopped completely and the sky cleared and it dawned on me how much of a beautiful day it actually was. The moment that I was taken back in it started thundering and storming even harder than it was before I went out so hard the power went out in the facility for a moment. For me it was powerful, reassuring and it made me believe that God was still with me. There were a lot of moments like that throughout my incarceration that let me know that I had something special and spiritual guarding me and carrying me through all those years outside of my own efforts. Isolation forces you to pay attention to these things. Administrative Seg was the worst, however I had some really amazing revelations in that time and that is one of the times in my life that I felt the Most High's presence, voice and saw His works.

Like I mentioned before, Seg was extremely cold. When I was forced there I didn't have much of anything. My clothes went missing and my commissary bag had just finished. I would stay warm by working out but there was no real getting past the cold of those walls. But I'm highly favored. One day when laundry came around to change our uniforms I noticed a new face checking the windows. It was a correctional officer that I'll refer to as Benny. Benny and I had had an interaction before when I was in D1-3 on a laundry day just like this one here. That day Benny was an asshole but so was I. I woke up out of my sleep from him banging and shouting through the bean shoot for laundry. When I went to give him my laundry he snatched it out of my hands and mugged me. I didn't respond well to that. He didn't respond well to my response.

"Aye bro you don't gotta snatch shit outta my hands and mug me. I didn't choose to be here, you're here by choice if you don't like your job, quit. You're free to walk out those door at any moment but you don't have to sit here and take your misery out on me"

"Wtf did you say?! Open the doors."

The doors opened and Benny was immediately in my face. I wasn't moved. I told him what I said again and assured him that I would beat the shit outta him if he tried me that day. He exploded, again I wasn't moved. Another inmate woke up and grabbed for me as another guard entered the room to grab Benny.

Now months later in Seg we meet again, on laundry day. This day was different though. Benny looked at me in awe and gave me 3 extra blankets, 3 pairs of socks and some long sleeves. Before telling me to Keep my head up and talk to God. From then on every time Benny was on shift during Administrative Seg, he would be sure to slide me 2 extra trays during chow time.

Another time I knew my HIgher power was listening to me deeply was with my first appointed attorney. Todd Tudley. This guy sucked, for real. But I literally asked God for this man to be my attorney because I would hear such good things about him from other inmates. This situation reassured me of something I had always known. I've always gotten exactly what I wanted in life, like literally. Whether it was good for me or bad for me, if I asked God for it I got it. It was humbling and frightening at the same time. And a big contributor to my sangfroid demeanor.

D1-2: A New Reality

When I left segregation, I was no longer the person I had been. The isolation had sharpened me, honing my focus to a razor's edge. I was still humble and kind, but empathy had become a distant luxury. My new reality began in D1-2, a 24-man dorm, a place unlike anything I had ever known. Here, the politics were intense, racial divides ran deep, and a strategically placed blind spot became an unofficial battleground where fights often went unnoticed by guards. Amid this chaos, I found kinship with other young men, all fighting battles of their own. We laughed, supported each other, and built a fragile camaraderie—a brotherhood forged in the crucible of confinement.

In D1-2, I met many significant people, though most never made it home. One of them was my boy Freddy. Locked up since he was sixteen, he was only nineteen when we met, facing several more years in pretrial detention. By the time he finally went to trial, he was twenty-three and sentenced to two consecutive twenty-three-year prison terms. Freddy had severe PTSD from a cartel kidnapping and lacked guidance, resources, or a fighting chance. But he had one of the most brilliant business minds I had ever seen, and his sense of humor never wavered. Freddy and I endured many ups and downs together, but his loyalty never wavered. We survived off each other's hustle, sending hundreds of dollars home from gambling to sustain ourselves when our loved ones couldn't provide. We stood together against all odds—guards, inmates, or whatever else came our way. Freddy is my brother in loyalty, always.

Another unforgettable figure in D1-2 was Antonio Brown, a terrifying yet gentle giant. He suffered from mental health issues that resembled Parkinson's disease, a result of being shot in the head twice. He had been incarcerated for years, and the guards were terrified of him. At 6'4" and ox-strong, he had the mind of a child. He called everyone "nephew" and truly believed that Beyoncé was his daughter and Boosie was his son. Brown had an animated smile and loved to play poker. He wasn't all there, but he was a good person. I don't know what happened to him, but Brown was part of every story in that dorm.

One day, while in D1-2, I saw a familiar face from the free world—my old friend Myles walked through the doors. We hadn't seen each other since middle school, and the shock on his face mirrored my own. He, too, was here on false charges that ultimately stole nearly three years of his life. In that time, he lost his relationships, his connection with his children, and everything he had once known. Myles was frequently moved, sent on CHAIN—transfers to distant county jails due to overcrowding. Despite this, we kept in touch through letters. Whenever he returned, he would do whatever was necessary to end up back in my dorm. Our shared letters and camaraderie helped us survive.

Hays County Jail was overcrowded and deliberately slow-moving in the courts. Twice a week, inmates were transferred to out-of-county facilities—Limestone, Eagle Pass, Burnet, Atascocita, and more. Some of these transfers were five to six hours away. We called it "Catching CHAIN." Nobody wanted to be on that list. It was brutal—being woken up aggressively at 2 AM, your belongings shoved into random trash bags, and then shackled for transport to a county where you had no charges, no family, and no contact. These transfers often led to lost property, broken relationships, and made communication with attorneys nearly impossible, further crippling any chance of a fair defense.

When transferred to another county, you had to be rebooked into their system, repeating the arrest and intake process all over again. You were dropped into a jail full of strangers, immediately an outsider. Sometimes, it took weeks before your attorney or loved ones could even locate you. Transfers created extreme risks for both inmates and guards, often leading to riots and standoffs. The guards loved it. The inmates, however, were traumatized by it, week after week.

Each time Myles returned, I felt relief. Seeing him meant he had survived yet another CHAIN transfer. His presence reminded me of the world we had been stolen from and the hope that maybe one day, we would make it back.

D1-2 became even more hellish when COVID-19 struck. We had no idea what it was—we only knew something terrible was happening when people around us started collapsing. Information was scarce. In jail, news barely trickled in, and we were given no protection. I caught COVID three times. The first time was the worst. I passed out on three separate occasions—once trying to use the restroom, again getting out of my bunk, and once more attempting to exercise. The virus tore through the jail like wildfire. Guards didn't acknowledge it until enough of them got sick and started calling off work. Only then did they tell us what was happening. But even then, we received no masks, no proper medical care—nothing. We were trapped with an invisible killer, completely defenseless.

Jail introduces you to people you wish you'd never met and those who stay with you forever. I encountered the best of both in those years caged in D1-2. In D1-2, I encountered two men I'll call Red and Snow. Both were tall, heavily tattooed, and had gang histories. Snow, with his frost-colored hair, was openly racist, but circumstances forced us to interact. Red, on the other hand, was a renewed Christian and became a lifelong friend. He believed so deeply in my fight for justice that when he was released, he advocated tirelessly for me, reaching out to Amy Kamp and MANO AMIGA, urging them to get involved. Myles did the same, speaking on news reports and at community events, building awareness to get me home.

Snow and I passed the time playing spades and chess, forming an odd but mutual respect. One day, he approached me with a revelation—he knew Rodney Reed, a man wrongfully convicted of murdering Stacey Stites in the 1990s. Reed was all over the news because the Innocence Project was fighting to stop his execution. Snow had done time with the real killer—a deputy who had confessed to murdering his wife, Stacey Stites. Caught between his loyalty to his gang and the truth, Snow wrestled with whether to speak up. Ultimately, he agreed to help. So I wrote a letter for him and sent it off the next morning. His information contributed to a stay of execution for Reed.

Snow's assistance helped him, too. He received support overcoming his own criminal charges and was able to return home. After his release, he kept in touch, calling me just to talk and tell me to stay strong. But not long after he got out, Snow was found dead in a hotel room. The official cause was an overdose, but Red and I suspected otherwise.

I stayed in D1-2 until COVID shut the world down. Over those years, I watched people come and go, experienced the crushing frustration of countless shakedowns that left us with lost or destroyed belongings, and endured relentless attempts by the system to break me—tampering with my mail, setting me up for fights, and destroying crucial legal documents. Yet, despite it all, I remained undeterred. D1-2 was a world of endless chaos, but within it, I found resilience, brotherhood, and the unwavering will to keep fighting for my freedom.

Jail is Jail

By the time I was released on bond, I had cycled through nearly every male dorm in that jail. I moved from D1-3 to D2-8, then D2-7, back to D1-3, then to Administrative Seg., D1-2, back to D1-3, D1-4, A1, to F1 when the new section of the jail opened, F4, back to F1, F3, and finally walked out of D4. My name had become notorious; guards generally despised me and made literal attempts on my life, and among inmates, I was either respected or reviled. Regardless of how I was viewed, I kept my mind focused on getting home. I reminded myself every day that this was not my world, and it was certainly not going to define the rest of my life.

Nonetheless I became cold. I was targeted and tired of it. The guards inevitably pushed me to a point, but I never broke. They set me up to be jumped on multiple occasions. And worse. If one jeopardized my physical well being and overall health. In one instance I was locked in a small van sized room known as the sally port, with a 6 '8 guy with AIDs that hated me because I beat him in chess months before. he was sent on the transfer list. I'll refer to him as GScott. GScott was incarcerated for murdering his girlfriend for allegedly giving him AIDs. After the incident he went on the run and was eventually locked down at what I'll say was a gas station where he had a shootout with the police before his arrest. GScott had been in our tank for a few days before being sent on a transfer list. Within those few days I beat him in chess and it apparently festered a secret hatred for me, however, in jail a person doesn't have to say much for you to see how they're coming.

Eventually it was known that there was a problem between me and GScott when I had to "get on his ass" for disrespecting me. We didn't fight that day though. My friend AJ stopped it because we were the only few black people in the tank and we had to "stick together". I was past that point. Later AJ grew past it too and almost spazzed out on GScott, but I stopped him that time. The next day GScott was sent on the transfer. Before he came back we learned GScott had AIDs and were relieved neither of us risked fighting him.

When he returned he sat in the hall and talked to Corporals for a while. Apparently about me. One of the corporals later came to my tank to call me to talk. Asking if it'll be a problem if he puts GScott in our tank. My response was;

"Why are you asking me, outta all the people in here, why'd you call me to ask that?"

He walked away. The next morning the doors opened and GScott was walking in. He had his shoes on and he was looking at me as I read my book. I immediately put my shoes on and the fight began. I punched GScott back into the sally port and immediately the guards locked us in that small room as I fought for my life. Once they noticed I was winning they opened the door and rushed the both of us, tasing and slamming us, then they took me to a separate room to try to talk about it. On another occasion I was moved to a tank where Mexican gang members were jumping black people on site. This was known information throughout the facility, Why? I couldn't tell you.

I was moved to this tank for questioning officer Isaiah Garcia for tampering with my mail. He didn't like my questions and quickly called several guards for back up as I conversed with him. When they came they surrounded me and he immediately told them to move me to F3, where it was known that Mexican gang members were jumping black people on site. Others in our tank warned and demanded that they don't move me over there for two reasons. I had done nothing wrong and I would most definitely be jumped if they moved me over there. Garcia and his corporal ignored, laughed and threatened to do the same to my friend Myles as he advocated against their decision.

When they took me to F3, they threw me in without any of my property. Unusual. Immediately I saw the eyes lurking. I was cool with whatever outcome at this point. I went to the door that separated the F3 and F4 dorm with a rec yard. DeVonte was on that side. We hadn't seen each other in years. We talked by that door for a bit catching up on life and family. Before we were done talking I said;

"Look bro they finna try to jump me, but don't crash out, over there just chill."

He didn't like that request, but I knew what was going on and to me it didn't make sense for the both of us to crash out behind this so I asked him not to.

From there I went to the guard to ask why my property wasn't brought in with me. He smirked. I then said, "you know they're gonna try to jump me right?". His response was, "Well you handled yourself pretty well with GScott." His condescending remark only made me more ready to punch, I just hoped nobody had any shanks on them. Most of these guys really couldn't fight and were not afraid to stab you if they could. Soon after I was locked in a cell with these same Mexican gang members. I immediately started punching and moving. We were in the cell for nearly 5 minutes as the guard stood by the locked door watching for a while before "calling it in". Once the door was opened the Mexican gang members tried to run out. I was in an ungodly rage and pulled the first one I could right back in and continued to whale on him, until I was again body slammed and jumped on by several guards. They let him walk out of the cell.

As they carried me out in cuffs my mind raced and I could see DeVonte at the rec yard window with the same race going on in his. I was moved back to the F1 the same dorm that I was moved out of to be jumped. When I returned the room was tense. No one was happy about what had just happened and now everyone was ready to choose violence immediately. The guards locked me in the same cell they threw me out of for the remainder of the day. I couldn't use the phone and I still had no access to my property. Myles had to contact my family about what had happened. That night was a terrible night for Hispanics in F1. All of the black people were literally looking for any one to retaliate against and they did more than once before breakfast came, jaws were shattered to say the least. It was Chaos that night and everyday moving forward.

As for me, the next morning I was greeted by two corporals, a captain, officer Garcia himself and the same guard that watched me get jumped. They took me to a small room with a camera to try to convince me to say that; me getting jumped was because of something that I had done to upset the other inmates. I almost slapped them.

"You people are crazy as hell. There is no way you think you're about to bring me into a small room with a camera and try to intimidate me into being your scapegoat for deliberately putting my life in danger. On more than one occasion now. **** you."

They then tried to make me sign a paper for punishment, I refused and they locked me back in my cell for another day. I was okay with it, at that point I had made up my mind. I'll surely die or kill a man in here before I give in to anything that is not of me or mine. Guard and inmate alike. I was already seen as a threat without every trying to be all these years now I was okay with being the apex predator in the room. And I did just that. I later came to find out that my friend Tae was jumped by the same Mexican gang too. From then on anytime a hispanic came in the dorm I would check them about it.

"Aye bro you Blast?" and if they said yes I would respond "Fasho, yo patnas jumped my lil bro, so look come to my cell i'm finna beat the shit outta you and take all your shit or you leave rn and I'm still take all your shit, you a gangster right?" My calm confidence was terrifying and I meant every word I said. It got so bad the hispanics in the dorm would start telling others as they were brought in to go talk to Cyrus in cell 23 before you put your stuff in a cell. In those days I became the worst person to try in the entire building. I didn't care about anything. Whenever I felt bothered I became the monster in the room. But I was no bully. I just reciprocated energy and let it be known that Cyrus is going to take it too far every chance he gets so you might as well not even take it there. I hated that version of myself.

Part II: Court & Attorneys

After five long months in jail, I was finally served my indictment papers and assigned a court-appointed attorney, Todd Dudley By this time I had been in fights, riots, dealt with unjust prejudice, and Administrative Segregation. My court appointed attorneys first words to me were,

"Wow, you really went for the big one, didn't you?"

Right then and there I had a bad feeling about him. But I had heard nothing but good things about the guy and his counsel. So much that I actually prayed he would be appointed to me and he was. He never even once told me how any conviction at all could affect my immigration status terribly, That became a harsh lesson of "Be careful what you wish for," I learned soon enough that just because he was a good attorney for others, that did not mean he would have the same care and passion for me and my situation. none the less it strengthened my spiritual resolve.

Court appearances were frequent but pointless, with hours spent in a freezing holding cell for endless resets. Each trip offered a brief glimpse of the outside world, and moments of music played by a sympathetic guard became precious escapes. Determined to take control of my fate, I began to educate myself on the law. I copied anything I could from fellow inmates and asked my loved ones for materials. I wrote letters and motions, seeking guidance and advocating for myself. I reached out to numerous advocacy groups like the NAACP, but their responses were always the same: they couldn't help unless I was already wrongfully convicted of Capital Murder and facing life without parole or the death sentence. I wrote to celebrities and athletes, hoping they would empathize with my struggle. I even wrote to higher courts about the injustices we were facing. I wrote so much those days that my hands would cramp up at night.

The process of self-education was grueling but empowering. Each legal document I deciphered and every piece of advice I received built my resolve. I learned to navigate the complexities of the justice system, armed with nothing but borrowed books and sheer determination. My cell became a makeshift law library, where nights were spent drafting motions and researching precedents, each letter I sent a lifeline cast into a sea of indifference.

After nearly two years of nothing and no progress, Dudley resigned from my case, his parting words a testament to his disinterest in my defense.

"Well, Cyrus, you're guilty... I'll tell you what, I haven't looked into your case, but if the judge makes me stay on, I'll look into it and see what I can do."

In that moment, I realized I wasn't a person with rights and loved ones in the eyes of the State and its actors. I was just a case number, an easy trade-off for a Caucasian man accused of similar crimes to get a lesser sentence. This same attorney would look my mom in the eyes on my court dates and ask; "what are you doing here?"

"Your son is never coming home," he said.

"Why don't you just convince him to take 45". A year after I came home he offered to write a letter of recommendation for me to go to law school. Right...

My next attorney, Playa P, had his own struggles and limitations, but he did enough to keep my case moving. Even though we had our differences, I genuinely believe that Playa P did everything within his power to help me through my plight, and for that, I am deeply grateful. His efforts, though imperfect, were still a lifeline in a storm that threatened to drown me. Yet, it was frustrating, almost maddening, to witness what his "everything" looked like in practice. I could see the gaps, the missed opportunities, and the untapped potential that I knew could have made a world of difference. I couldn't shake the feeling that so much more could have been done, that the path to my freedom and redemption could have been smoother, swifter, less tortuous if only he had pushed a little harder, seen a little clearer, cared a little more.

But in this harsh world, I've come to understand that not everyone will see you—truly see you for who you are or who you're striving to become. Your vision, your dreams, your desperate sense of urgency are yours alone, burning inside you with an intensity that no one else can fully comprehend. It's a lonely, isolating realization, one that forces you to grapple with the painful truth: not everyone shares the same passion for your life that you do. People can walk beside you, offer a hand, or even carry you for a while, but they will never carry the same weight in their hearts as you do in yours. They can support your journey, but they cannot live it. This understanding was sobering. I learned that while others can help, the fire that drives me must be my own, fanned and fueled by my unwavering belief in the vision that only I can see.

Only, I too knew that my vision was blurred by my trauma, but nevertheless I pushed through and kept going.

Part III: Chess & Trial

My trial was a nightmarish ordeal, a surreal distortion of justice that felt more like a theater of the absurd than a pursuit of truth. The jury pool was a stark reminder of the deep-seated racial biases in the system. Out of over 400 potential jurors, only two were Black, and none of them could truly be considered my peers. The Prosecutor, Ralph Guerrero's opening statement shocked my nerves beyond belief.

I felt the weight of this injustice from the start, knowing that my fate rested in the hands of people who might never understand my reality. The state's case against me was as fragile as a house of cards, yet it was being propped up by a series of procedural manipulations and outright fabrications.

The evidence presented was riddled with holes, gaps so glaring they should have been impossible to overlook. Yet, the District Attorney, Ralph Guerrero, had the audacity to turn those gaps into his twisted narrative. He opened his argument with a jigsaw puzzle of a pistol projected on the screen, pieces blatantly missing. "I want you all to look at this," he said with a smirk.

"There are a bunch of pieces missing, right? But you can all tell that's a firearm. Well, that's what we have here with this case. There's a lot that we don't know, but based on what we think happened, you will be able to convict Mr. Gray of Capital Murder."- **Ralph Guerrero**

His brazen words almost made me throw up on the spot, the sheer audacity of convicting someone on a 'what we think happened' premise was nauseating.

As the trial dragged on, that same small man, who seemed to swell with his own self-righteousness, leapt up beside me in his closing statement nearly a month later. He pointed directly at my face, his voice rising to a fevered pitch, spitting venom with every word.

"LOOK AT HIM, JUST LOOK AT HIM! HE'S A ****ING MURDERER! HOW CAN YOU NOT SEE THAT? LOOK AT HIM!!"

His desperation to vilify me was palpable, almost comical if it weren't so terrifying. At that moment, my mind darkened with violent thoughts. In my head, I became a murderer—*his* murderer, as I fantasized about ending his miserable existence right there, silencing him forever.

But instead of reacting, I sat there, stone-faced and emotionless, my eyes fixed forward while my heart and head pounded, pumping fury through my veins. It took everything in me to keep my composure, to not let the fire burning inside me spill out. I knew that any show of emotion would be twisted against me, used to further the narrative they were so desperately trying to construct. So I sat, a cauldron of rage and fear, holding onto the only thing I felt I had left—myself.

The bizarre truths of the state's broken and shaky case continued. Crucial interviews and reports had mysteriously disappeared, lost by none other than the lead detective, Sandra Spreigel herself and SMPD. Her admissions of incompetence should have cast doubt on the entire investigation, but they were glossed over, dismissed as trivial errors. Even their own experts conceded that Devonte's cell phone and mine—the biggest part of their case—was miles away from the crime scene at the time of the alleged offense. A fact that should have exonerated me and him immediately. There was no DNA evidence matching DeVonte's or mine. No murder weapon, no eye witness account. No way to know if Devonte and I were even ever at the crime scene at the time of the incident or ever. The investigation was botched and the police bias had state actors too far gone.

Dr. Kim Rossmo's Work on Police Bias

Dr. Kim Rossmo is a criminologist known for his expertise in geographic profiling, a method used to track criminals based on the locations of their crimes. His work has also touched on issues of cognitive bias in policing and how these biases can negatively impact criminal investigations.

Rossmo has studied how confirmation bias, tunnel vision, and other cognitive biases can lead police to make critical investigative errors. His research highlights how these biases can cause law enforcement officers to:

1. **Focus on a single suspect too early** – Investigators may become fixated on a suspect despite weak or contradictory evidence, ignoring alternative leads.
2. **Disregard exculpatory evidence** – Once officers develop a theory, they may unconsciously reject or downplay evidence that contradicts it.
3. **Over-rely on intuition rather than systematic methods** – Instead of using data-driven techniques, officers may let personal beliefs or hunches drive their investigations.
4. **Ignore or misinterpret geographic patterns** – His expertise in geographic profiling has shown that investigators sometimes ignore the spatial behaviors of criminals, leading to misdirected searches.

Negative Effects on Investigations and Cases

Rossmo's research has demonstrated that bias in policing can lead to wrongful arrests and convictions, as well as unsolved cases. Some key consequences include:

- **Wrongful convictions** – When investigators ignore alternative suspects or exculpatory evidence, innocent people can be convicted.
- **Cold cases and missed perpetrators** – A narrow focus on the

wrong suspect can allow the real perpetrator to continue committing crimes.

- **Public distrust in law enforcement** – When cases are mishandled due to bias, it erodes trust between the police and the communities they serve.

Rossmo has argued for the use of structured investigative techniques, including geographic profiling, data-driven decision-making, and awareness training to combat cognitive biases in policing.

1. The Wrongful Conviction of David Milgaard (Canada, 1969)

- **Background**: David Milgaard was wrongfully convicted of the rape and murder of a nurse, Gail Miller, in Saskatchewan. He spent **23 years in prison** before DNA evidence exonerated him in 1992.
- **Bias Involved**:
  - **Tunnel Vision**: Police fixated on Milgaard early in the investigation, despite unreliable witness statements and weak forensic evidence.
  - **Confirmation Bias**: Investigators interpreted ambiguous statements as confessions rather than considering alternative interpretations.
- **Rossmo's Findings**:
  - If investigators had used objective, structured methods, including geographic profiling, they might have identified the actual perpetrator—**Larry Fisher**, a serial rapist who lived in the area.
  - The case demonstrated how cognitive biases could result in ignoring exculpatory evidence and lead to wrongful imprisonment.

2. The Wrongful Conviction of Steven Avery (Wisconsin, 1985)

- **Background**: Steven Avery was wrongfully convicted of sexual assault and spent **18 years in prison** before being exonerated by DNA evidence.
- **Bias Involved**:
  - **Presumptive Guilt**: Local police believed Avery was guilty due to his past minor offenses, leading them to ignore contradictory evidence.
  - **Disregard for Alternate Suspects**: The actual rapist, Gregory Allen, continued committing crimes while police focused on Avery.
- **Rossmo's Analysis**:
  - The investigation lacked **data-driven approaches**, such as geographic profiling, which could have directed law enforcement toward Gregory Allen.
  - The case illustrated how law enforcement can **shape evidence** to fit a predetermined suspect rather than following objective investigative methods.

3. The Portland "Serial Killer" Investigation (Oregon, 2000s)

- **Background**: In the early 2000s, Portland police believed they had a serial killer targeting women in the city.
- **Bias Involved**:
  - **Pattern Bias**: Police assumed the deaths were connected and overlooked other explanations.
  - **Cognitive Fixation**: They dismissed alternative causes of death and other potential suspects.
- **Rossmo's Contribution**:
  - His geographic profiling research suggested that the police

were **forcing a pattern** where none existed.

- The supposed "serial killings" were actually **unrelated deaths**, and the real threats to the community were ignored due to misplaced focus.

4. The D.C. Sniper Case (2002)

- **Background**: John Allen Muhammad and Lee Boyd Malvo carried out a series of sniper attacks in the Washington, D.C. area.
- **Bias Involved**:
  - **Racial Profiling**: Police initially searched for a "lone white male in a white van," ignoring reports describing a dark-colored car with two occupants.
  - **Fixation on a Specific Crime Pattern**: Investigators assumed the shooter was acting alone and dismissed key evidence linking the crimes.
- **Rossmo's Perspective**:
  - A **data-driven approach** using geographic profiling could have helped police identify the suspects sooner.
  - Bias in suspect profiling delayed their capture, prolonging public fear and additional attacks.

Lessons from Rossmo's Case Studies

1. **Tunnel Vision Leads to Wrongful Convictions** – Investigators must remain open to new evidence rather than forcing facts to fit a suspect.
2. **Misidentification of Crime Patterns Wastes Resources** – Geographic profiling and data analysis can help avoid misleading assumptions.
3. **Ignoring Alternative Suspects Lets Criminals Stay Free** – Systematic investigative methods should be prioritized over

intuition-based policing.

Rossmo continues to advocate for **bias awareness training, structured decision-making models, and geographic profiling tools** to prevent these mistakes in future investigations

The Show Goes On

The courtroom was far from a place of fairness. My judge, the very person entrusted with ensuring justice, spent the majority of my Capital Murder trial engrossed in Candy Crush on his phone. It was a blatant display of apathy, a clear sign that my life meant little more than a passing distraction. The prosecutor, Ralph Guerrero, was relentless, treating my friends—who had come forward to support me—as if they were the ones on trial. He twisted their words, painted them as liars and thieves, and pushed some of them into the position of hostile witnesses, where every word was weaponized against me and themselves. No different from SMPD aggressively botching the investigation of our case.

Through it all, I was forced to sit in silence, my emotions suppressed by the iron grip of my attorney, Playa P. His instructions were clear: "Don't let the jury see you show any emotions." It was a cruel demand, stripping me of my humanity in the very moment when I needed it most. Every fiber of my being screamed to defend myself, to stand up against the lies and the deceit, but I had to bury it all deep inside. The trial was not just an attack on my freedom—it was an attack on my soul.

So instead, I took notes of everything, word for word, to the best of my ability and forced him to ask questions he otherwise wouldn't have. Despite the clear uncertainty, my trial ended in a mistrial due to COVID-19, after nearly a month of the prosecutor painting a picture that didn't fit. The fight for my freedom was far from over, but I was determined to see it through. After the trial, it felt like I had another mountain to climb and only two choices: climb it or destroy it. I chose to blow that bitch up. I was fed up, and I wasn't going down without a fight. In those days I became the bear constantly waiting to be poked, not shying away from any opportunity to release my pain and anger on any poor soul willing to poke. All the while I remained with a tunnel vision, looking for any way out and bottling everything else deep inside.

Chapter IV:

Welcome Home

"The only real prison is fear, and the only real freedom is freedom from fear."
- Aung San Suu Kyi

Part I: Looking Back

In March 2018, when I was arrested, I had no inkling that nearly five years of my life would be consumed by a jail cell, devoid of a conviction. As someone with a clean record, the notion that such a fate could befall me seemed distant, yet it's a reality many endure, each story a reminder of the capriciousness of justice. I often reflected on the lives disrupted by a system that seemed more focused on punishment than truth. Now, almost seven years later, my case remains unresolved, but I refuse to let time slip away without purpose.

Every day spent in limbo has taught me the value of resilience and the power of hope. I've channeled my experiences into a mission to advocate for others who find themselves ensnared in the same unforgiving web. I've witnessed firsthand how easily lives can be shattered, and it has ignited a fire within me to raise awareness about wrongful incarceration. While the world outside continued to move forward, I became determined to transform my pain into purpose. I write, speak, and connect with those who have faced similar struggles, striving to create a community of support and empowerment. In doing so, I aim to reclaim not just my own narrative, but the narratives of countless others who have been silenced, ensuring that our stories echo beyond the confines of those walls and resonate with a larger movement for justice and change. Individuals like Bobby J Harper, Davonte Miller, Antione Benson and Freddy.

Bobby J Harper was wrongfully accused of murder by the same system and prosecution team in Hays County that attempted to strip my life away. He is currently still serving a prison sentence, 20 something years later for a crime he did not commit. Antione– or 5th– was sentenced to 40 plus years for a crime with falsified evidence and gang testimony. He is still actively fighting to overturn his cruel sentencing. Davonte Miller, known as Tae is serving a 55 year sentence for a murder in self defense. And you already know about Freddy. I still talk to these men to this day and support them however I can while we fight to bring them and others home from this cruel Texas system.

Inside those county walls, I was confronted with the brutal truth of our justice system—its severe inadequacies and injustices were glaring. From the indifferent court-appointed attorneys to the harsh conditions of pretrial incarceration, it was clear: this system is designed to break you. I quickly became an advocate—not just for myself, but for those suffering alongside me in Hays County Jail and in the courtrooms. In pretrial detention, your voice is silenced, and your rights are trampled. You're seen as guilty until proven innocent, treated as if your crime was witnessed firsthand by everyone around you.

Communication with lawyers, especially court-appointed ones, was a relentless struggle. Letters went unanswered, calls ignored, and many inmates hadn't seen or heard from their lawyer in months, even years. The system grinds you down, stripping you of your dignity, your rights, and your hope. It's not just the correctional officers who treat you this way; medical and mental health staff are often complicit. The jail system thrives on this dehumanization, denying access to basic legal materials, while lawyers and judges often dismiss defendants' claims.

Medical neglect was rampant in Hays County Jail. I witnessed people suffer profoundly from both medical and mental health neglect. I saw Melvin Nicholas nearly die twice because of it. I, too, experienced severe medical neglect, resulting in long-term health issues I'm still grappling with. I came home with new allergies, physical pains, worsening eyesight, and deep psychological scars. The hardest part of my incarceration was the mental anguish, the psychological torture that the system takes pride in. It grinds you down until you either tap out or die. I did neither, at least physically, but the internal and psychological deaths were countless. I lost so much of myself that I hadn't realized how much of me had died during that time. This book's metaphor speaks to the concept of rebirth through sacrifice. Each "man" that is killed symbolizes an old version of the self that must die for the new self to be born. It's a process of letting go of past identities, destructive mindsets, and emotional baggage. The sacrifice is not in the physical but in the emotional and mental, paving the way for true transformation.

It was within this unrelenting nightmare that I unlocked new levels of strength within myself, and discovered a determination not just to survive but to fight back against the system that sought to destroy me. Each day became a battle, not just against the walls that confined me, but against the psychological warfare that threatened to consume my soul. I learned to navigate the intricate web of oppression, to find small victories in the face of overwhelming odds. The battle is far from over, but I am no longer the man they tried to break. I am something stronger, something they will never understand or defeat. Despite the scars that remain. So much was lost in those years and I was just beginning to find out just how much was taken from me.

Part II: 2022

The months that followed my trial plunged me into a darkness deeper than I ever imagined. It was a suffocating abyss, where every breath felt like a struggle against the weight of injustice that threatened to crush me entirely. Despite the small voice deep within me, whispering that all the battles I fought, the heartbreaks I endured, and the mental anguish I suffered hadn't been in vain, I felt an overwhelming sense of defeat. It was as if the very essence of who I was had been stripped away, leaving behind a hollow shell that only existed to endure the torment that lay ahead.

I anxiously awaited a bond hearing, clinging to the fragile hope that maybe, just maybe, there would be some semblance of justice. But as the days dragged on, hope began to feel like a distant memory. Each day was a brutal test of survival. I faced violent clashes with guards and inmates, each altercation a bitter reminder of the world that sought to destroy me. Yet, within this chaos, something unexpected happened. I discovered friendships that transcended those cell walls—bonds so strong that they would last a lifetime, creating a lifeline that kept me tethered to some semblance of humanity.

I'll never forget how Isaiah Garcia set me up to be jumped by a Mexican prison gang because I questioned him about tampering with my mail, a question that turned into a room full of guards standing around me, myself and I. Months later, after my release, he murdered Joshua Wright and walked free, after shooting Joshua, an unarmed shackled man in an emergency room, several times in the back. Violence and betrayal were constant companions.

Going through the system, you begin to develop a deep, burning hatred for law enforcement. It's not the kind of resentment that stems from a single incident, but a festering wound that opens wider with every encounter, every interaction, every soul-crushing moment they inflict on you. You start to see through the cracks in their polished façade, noticing their two-faced, cowardly tactics designed to break you down and strip away any remaining sense of dignity.

These so-called protectors of the peace, along with their allies, have brought nothing but pain and trauma into my life and the lives of those I care about. And for what? There was no justifiable reason, no legitimate cause for the havoc they wreaked. They hounded us both inside and outside the jail walls, relentless in their pursuit of power and control. The most infuriating part of it all was their unyielding determination to cover up their wrongdoings, to cleanse their hands of the blood they spilled, and to twist the narrative in their favor. They would rather justify their wickedness than face the truth and right their wrongs.

In all that I endured, not a single apology was offered. Not a hint of remorse or acknowledgment of the torment they put me through. Why would there be? To them, I'm not a person worthy of compassion or justice—I'm their "bad guy," their favorite "monster." In their eyes, I'm the one to blame, the one to demonize, the one they can lock away and forget about. But what they fail to realize is that their cruelty only revealed their flaws and forced me to pay attention in ways I probably otherwise wouldn't have.

During those months, I became less compassionate, losing empathy and growing increasingly reckless. Yet, in the presence of my loved ones and newfound support, I held on to some remnants of myself—calm and kind.

My bond hearing was delayed for months after the trial. My attorney, Playa P, was pessimistic, pushing me to postpone it until January 2023. It was November 2022, five months since my trial had ended. My family showed up in force, joined by supporters from MANO AMIGA, including Melinda, a juror from my first trial who had written a compelling article in the Texas Observer about the injustices I had faced. Amy Kamp, Karen Muñoz and MANO AMIGA, literally hand delivered my entire bond packet to Playa P

Professor Matt Clair of Stanford wrote a letter of support after supporting me tirelessly from the outside, and

Shannon FitzPatrick, whom I had never met or known anything about at the time, offered her home as a place for me to stay if I was granted bond. Despite all this, my attorney seemed determined to dissuade me because he didn't believe the judge would grant my motion to reduce my bond. But not before trying to convince my suffering mother and father to do so, they refused. I also refused his advice to delay and, against all odds, was home before Christmas.

Part III: Adjusting

Walking out of those gates felt surreal. In the car, I instinctively sat in the center of the back seat, as if still shackled in a dog catcher. I was institutionalized. My mind raced, and my heart pounded. "You can relax; you're not in jail anymore," my mom said. But believing it took time. Years later I still wake up sometimes surprised to be outside of those walls.

Coming home felt like stepping into an entirely new world, but the old wounds were far from healed. Every breath of freedom was tainted by the reminders of the years I'd lost. My body had changed—newfound allergies plagued me, my eyesight had worsened, and my lower back ached constantly from those countless nights spent on cement and metal beds. The excruciating wisdom teeth pain was an ever-present companion, as my jaw slowly realigned itself—a painful reminder of the time that had slipped away.

I returned to society without a legal identity. When I was arrested, the police confiscated my wallet, stripping me of everything I had—my social security card, my permanent residency card—everything that proved I existed in this world. None of it was ever returned to me. Instead, I later discovered that all my personal information had somehow ended up on the dark web, a chilling violation that left me vulnerable and exposed. The nightmare continued when I realized the bureaucratic labyrinth I was trapped in: I couldn't get a driver's license because I didn't have my social security card, and I couldn't get my social security card without identification. I found myself in the absurd position of being an expired immigrant in the very country I had called home, with no proof of who I was, and still out on bond for Capital Murder.

Shannon and Ron's house was like a sanctuary on a hill, overlooking the town below. It was peaceful, almost surreal—a stark contrast to the chaos I had left. Many nights, I would stand on their balcony, gazing out at the world, my mind struggling to process the reality of my newfound freedom. But even in this serene environment, the shadows of my past lingered. Old habits, forged in the crucible of incarceration, refused to let go. I still showered with my shoes on, a reflex from years in incarcerated, and I often caught myself washing clothes and dishes in the bathroom sink, unable to shake the routines that had once been essential for survival.

Amy Kamp, MANO AMIGA, Pastor Darius Todd, Kecia and the people who made up my village, supported me through this bewildering transition. They wanted to help, to lift me out of the darkness that clung to me, but I was still broken mentally, trapped in the trauma that had become my constant companion. I didn't let them help me as much as they wanted to, lost in my own pain and the overwhelming shock of the world outside. I spent countless hours alone, finding a fragile peace in riding a bike that Amy had gifted me, sitting in parks to smoke weed, and letting music drown out the noise in my head. When I wasn't seeking solace in these quiet moments, I turned to fleeting relationships and vices, grasping for anything that might numb the pain and silence the anger that simmered just beneath the surface.

I felt an urgent need to kill the old me, believing that if I didn't, it would consume everything around me. But in my efforts to destroy that part of myself, I was the one being consumed. I became increasingly disconnected from reality, believing I had to control not just my fate but the fate of those around me. The weight of this burden was unbearable, and yet I carried it alone, too afraid to seek help, too consumed by my own darkness to let anyone in.

During this time, I was still trapped in the legal system, in and out of court, awaiting a second trial. My life was a series of constraints—an 11 PM curfew, an ankle monitor that tracked my every move, regular check-ins with my pretrial officer, and a no-contact order that kept me away from many of my closest friends. The State of Texas loomed over me like a dark cloud, with officers following me while I rode my bike and patrol cars staking out Shannon's street, their presence a constant reminder that I was still not free.

The weight of it all was silently killing me. Night after night, I barely made it home before curfew, my mind racing with plans to escape the stronghold that the State of Texas had on me. I had been hit by a car during this time—another incident in a series of desperate, reckless attempts to outrun the past. I did everything but seek help, refusing to confront the PTSD that was slowly unraveling my mind and spirit.

I lived at Shannon and Ron's for over a year. During that time, my case was dismissed in a cowardly way. Amidst the chaos, I found my Twin Flame and her love became the beginning of my healing.

Chapter V:

Fighting for Freedom

"Our lives begin to end the day we become silent about things that matter."
— **Martin Luther King Jr.**

Part I: Intentional Delivery

The months following my release were a whirlwind of relentless battles, each day feeling like a new round in a never-ending fight. Out on bond and awaiting a second trial, I spent another seven grueling months entangled in the justice system's web, where every step forward was met with resistance. Playa P remained my attorney during this period, but our relationship was anything but smooth. Tension simmered between us, often boiling over into outright conflict. He believed he knew what was best for me, basing his judgments on the mere three hours he had spent advocating for me during a nearly month long trial. I was left feeling misunderstood and frustrated, but I couldn't deny that he had done what he felt was his best. For that, I offer him thanks, though deep down, I had hoped for more—a resolution, a sense of justice, something beyond the endless struggle. I mean this man looked me in the eyes and said; "maybe I could've argued that there was no probable cause to arrest you in the first place," after 5 years in jail and a Capital Murder trial. How would you feel about his counsel?

During this tumultuous time, I refused to be silenced. I became a relentless advocate, determined to shed light on the gross injustices endured by people like DeVonte Amerson, Myles Martin, Bobby J. Harper and countless others trapped in the same merciless systems. Inevitably putting an even larger target on my back.

I spoke out on every platform available, from podcasts to public events, including the State Capitol, where I tried to shake the foundations of a system that seemed impervious to change. One encounter with then-Senator Whittmire remains etched in my memory, a stark reminder of the indifference of those in power. My good friend Myles and I stood before the Commission on Jail Standards Committee, speaking our truth, only to be met with blatant disrespect, unlike any other speakers that day. By senator Whittmire himself. He believed we were at fault and that we had to have done something to have been wrapped up in the system that way. He was clearly bothered by our presence and even more uncomfortable with our message. So instead of listening he chose to attack two victims of his systems, emulous in his arrogance and disdain of these two black men from Houston.

Now that Whittmire is the Mayor of Houston, my fear for the city runs deep. Some people will never understand, relate to, or empathize with the lives and experiences of people like Myles and me. They've never known struggle—never woken up hungry with the lights out, never worked four jobs around the clock just to support their families. Their encounters with police have never been anything less than pleasant. How could they possibly relate? They are nothing like us, yet they control policies and rules that impact and affect only us.

I fought tirelessly to reason with people who seemed to hold the power to make a difference, including my own counsel Playa P. Yet, time and again, it felt like I was not only battling the State of Texas but also the very person who was supposed to be in my corner. Playa P dismissed my suggestions as ridiculous, only to later admit that he could have argued the same points himself, months down the line. The nights I spent in my cell, painstakingly handwriting motions and legal documents, felt like exercises in futility. My efforts were dismissed by my attorney before they could even be heard in open court, but I refused to accept the same treatment while free. My voice would not be silenced; my fight would not be in vain. So I made sure to get on his ass every chance I got, respectfully of course, until I absolutely couldn't anymore.

Our disagreements reached a boiling point, culminating in me demanding that Playa P "GTFO MY CASE!" The tension between us had reached an irreparable level, and the following week, we had a hearing for him to officially withdraw as my attorney. The Judge denied his withdrawal advocating for his "good works", so did the new Assistant District Attorney Gregg Cox, who knew nothing about my case or Playa P's "work"-- ADA Cox later went out of his way to assault me in open court several months later. Following that my disputes with Playa P continued until he called me the night before the court hearing to determine the date of my second trial to say he could no longer be a part of my defense. GREAT!!

Only it was terrible timing for him to notify me of this. I had a very important hearing just hours later. So that night in my panic and mixed emotions of what would come the next morning, I wrote a Motion requesting the judge to dismiss my case with prejudice due to my speedy trial rights being violated. I brought up the clear discrepancies in my trial as well as indisputable evidence of the States deliberate delay of my case pre and post release, outlining major violations of my right to speedy trial among other things. Then I wrote a letter to the judge.

During that hearing, I presented the motion and letter to the judge that I had written the night before, To my surprise, the judge agreed with my argument but rather than granting my motion, he warned the District Attorney that if they didn't resolve the matter before my next hearing—another reset away—, he would grant my motion, again I was cheated. For a brief moment, it felt like justice was within reach. But once again, the system failed me. The State of Texas, ever cunning, maneuvered to have my case dismissed WITHOUT prejudice through another judge while mine was on vacation, leaving me with an open Capital Murder case pending further investigation looming over my head and on my name indefinitely.

"Freedom is never voluntarily given by the oppressor; it must be demanded by the oppressed." — **Martin Luther King Jr.**

Never forget, Freedom isn't free. Before this clear miscarriage of justice, a newly graduated attorney named Ricky T stepped in and offered to help me. Ricky T was a beacon of hope in a landscape filled with despair. He amended my motion, making it nearly bulletproof, and assured me that he would be held in contempt before he allowed me to go unheard. I believed him. For the first time in what felt like forever, I believed that real justice might be within my grasp. However, the State of Texas had other plans. By law, the defense must inform the State of their arguments and motions before hearings so that the State can prepare. This rule, of course, doesn't apply the other way around.

Ricky T had to disclose our strategy, and upon realizing the strength of our amended motion, the State scrambled to formulate their own. They moved to dismiss the case without prejudice before our motion could be heard in court, ensuring that I remained in their grip. If my motion had been granted, it would have been akin to being found NOT GUILTY at trial—a level of justice that was clearly too much for them to allow.

Following my so-called "freedom," the fight continued, though the battlefield had shifted. I attended court for those still incarcerated, wrote pieces to expose the truth about the justice system, and kept DeVonte's struggle at the forefront of my mind. He remained incarcerated for the same crimes I had been "freed" from, so I couldn't let up—not now. But this fight was different and much bigger. I wasn't alone anymore; I had allies, which meant DeVonte had allies too. I had to trust this support if I wanted to help anyone else. But with newfound allies came new enemies, and the battle was far from over.

Detectives followed me around like shadows, I found a bug in my car, and every time I was pulled over, it felt like a life or death situation. Officers would say things like; "You know how this goes, you've done a lot of time before." Even worse they would know me by name before ever asking for my ID or anything and they wouldn't be shy about making that clear.

I felt bound to my fate, forever the villain. When you're finding recording devices hidden intentionally in your personal spaces it's easy to feel this way. My life had become a frightening conspiracy story as I became more and more unstable. I often say "the movie's gonna be crazy" to my close friends, because my life thus far has been just that.

One incident still haunts me night and day. My Twin Flame and I were pulled over while headed to her hometown for a birthday dinner. She was asleep in the passenger seat when I noticed the flashing lights behind us. I immediately woke her up.

"Baby, we're getting pulled over, call Karen".

I was terrified because she was here and I knew all the things that could go wrong because I was Cyrus Gray. I exited the highway and pulled over at a gas station hoping to at least have some safety with public eyes on us. As I parked my car and unlocked my phone to find Karen's number the shouts of police snatched our attention. We looked up to see we were surrounded by flashing lights and dozens of officers, all with guns drawn, aimed directly at my vehicle.

The tension in the air was fervent, thick enough to cut through with a knife. It felt like time had frozen as we sat there, hearts racing, adrenaline coursing through our veins. The harsh glare of the red, white and blue lights illuminated our faces, casting long shadows across the dashboard, and I could see the fear in my Twin Flame's eyes as we stared at each other—an expression that still echoes in my mind.

Her usually bright demeanor dimmed, replaced by a vulnerability that pierced my heart like a shard of glass. In that moment, I realized how precarious our situation truly was; the weight of the officers' weapons felt like a literal manifestation of the power imbalance we faced. Their voices barked orders, blending into a clatter of authority that engulfed us, while we remained frozen, paralyzed by uncertainty and fear, unsure of what would happen next. I could sense the collective anxiety radiating from those surrounding us, a wild energy that seemed to anticipate violence as if it were a storm about to break. And all I could think was; "F**k shes right here".

"Cyrus Gray, put your hands where I can see them!"

Their voices booming like thunder. I sat in stunned silence, my mind racing, but all I could focus on were her soft prayers for our lives, whispered in a shaky voice beside me. They demanded I open the door and exit the vehicle with my hands up. I looked into her eyes, a mirror of fear and concern, and slowly did as they asked, praying fervently that she wouldn't be harmed in the midst of my chaos.

As I cautiously walked toward the officers with my hands raised, I felt the weight of their glares, each officer's weapon aimed directly at my face. "Please put your guns away, my girlfriend is in the car," I begged meekly, my voice trembling with desperation. But instead of compassion, I was met with hostility. I was shaken up, thrown into the back of a squad car, multiple pairs of handcuffs biting into my wrists as they shouted at me, demanding to know where the drugs and weapons were hidden in my car—things that simply did not exist. "Who are you hiding in there?!" they wailed, their accusations echoing in the confines of my mind.

Tears streamed down my face as I pleaded with them, "Please, put your guns away! My girlfriend is in the car!" They didn't care. I screamed, feeling utterly helpless again. Trapped in that dark space, I banged my body against the metal walls of the squad car, a wasted cry for mercy as I rocked back and forth, desperate to get their attention, to break out or die trying, desperate to protect the love of my life sitting alone in the passenger seat of my car, surrounded by armed officers. They pulled her out of the car with guns in her face and forced her onto the ground. That story didn't end well. I thank God every day that it didn't end worse, that we both made it out alive, our spirits scarred but unbroken, a testament to our strength and resilience amidst such harrowing chaos.

In the aftermath, we were left shaken, grappling not only with the fear of that night but also with the realization that our lives could be so easily upended by a system that seemed to thrive on intimidation and violence. The memory of that confrontation still lingers, a haunting reminder of how quickly things can spiral out of control, leaving scars that take much longer to heal. I had just come back from visiting Professor Matthew Clair at Stanford University the day before.

Part II: Take a Second

Before we move forward to the next chapter of this story, I need to take a moment to reflect on the pain and grief that come with incarceration by opening up some memories that still sting to this day.

Pretrial incarceration is a harrowing experience, often defined by overcrowded, unsanitary conditions, lack of medical care, and inadequate mental health support. The isolation, mistreatment from both staff and fellow inmates, and the constant uncertainty can eat away at your mind. The worst part is the waiting—the endless stretch of time where you have no idea what's happening with your case or your life. Many are locked up simply because they can't afford bail, and some are innocent, trapped in a system that profits off human despair.

The toll on mental and physical health is brutal, and it doesn't stop with the person incarcerated—it spills over to your loved ones. Family ties weaken, and the pain of being separated from them becomes unbearable. What made it worse in my case was that those I cared about most had to make hard choices, like withholding certain painful truths just to protect me. It was their way of helping me survive, though in reality, the hurt found its way to me eventually in even worse ways.

For me, that realization hit hardest when I learned about the death of my childhood dog, Snowflake. I didn't find out until seven months after it happened. Snowflake, a bulky white pitbull with a pink and black nose, was my DAWG. My brother left him with us when he went off to college, and Snowflake and I pretty much went through highschool together. We even got arrested together once in Houston. Crazy story, I had a warrant for a traffic violation, and Snowflake, just a carefree dog, ended up hogtied with a muzzle in the back of a police car alongside me. We gave each other this look—both of us caught up in a situation that sucked. He was a loyal, loving dog with a player-like swagger. When he died from cancer, it was like losing a part of my youth, and the fact that no one told me until months later was devastating.

Another painful memory is missing my little sister's high school graduation. I couldn't be there, so my friend Jamahl Johnson stepped in for me. He stayed with my mom and helped her prepare for the big day, even attending the ceremony in my place. Jamahl and I hadn't been in touch for a while due to my situation, but when we finally connected, it was like no time had passed. We talked for almost an hour, laughing and encouraging each other, squeezing life into every minute of those 15-minute calls. But a few days later, when I tried to reach him again, I got nothing—no answer, no voicemail. I didn't find out until months later that Jamahl had died in a car accident shortly after our last conversation. That news hit harder than Tyson in his prime. That pain—like so many others—stayed bottled inside me, festering quietly.

Jamahl was one of the best people I've ever known. He had this infectious energy—full of light and positivity. He was the guy everyone wanted to be around, with the cleanest waves and the best dance moves at any party. His house was the first place my parents let me sleep over. We grew up together, shared everything—the good, the bad, and the dumb—with no regrets. Losing him broke something in me, and to this day, I still carry the weight of his loss.

These moments—losing Snowflake, missing my sister's graduation, and losing Jamahl—are just a few of the countless ways incarceration fractures your life. You're not only locked away physically but cut off emotionally, mentally, and spiritually. The outside world keeps moving, and you miss it all. You miss weddings, birthdays, funerals—moments you can never get back. But somehow, through all of it, you have to stay strong, not just for yourself but for everyone who needs you on the outside. I became their comfort, their listening ear, even as I was being torn apart inside.

Chapter VI:

Heroes & Villains

A strange man threw a car jack through my windshield as a friend and I drove on the feeder road...

If there is one thing I learned from the fight for my freedom, it is just how accurate it was when they said **The State of Texas vs. Cyrus Lua Gray III**. The efforts to destroy me and my peers were tireless, and they were working. Following the burglary of my actual innocence, I went to my proceeding judge's courtroom to affirm my disgust in what happened, and he said, "Sorry, son, there's nothing I can do now." So I was left with the monster on my back everywhere I went, a relentless specter haunting my every step. I felt like the District Attorney's and the police's favorite target, a scapegoat in their twisted game of power. Each time I walked past an officer or entered a courtroom, I could sense the eyes on me, judging, mocking, and relishing in my torment. It was a suffocating reality, as if I were perpetually trapped in a spotlight that illuminated my scars for all to see, while the real villains lurked in the shadows, untouched by the very justice they claimed to uphold.

To my peers, I was the hero, the one that made it out. And then turned around to throw the rope for others to do the same. They had no idea what my life had become, how the shadows of my past still loomed over me like a relentless storm. I even had people that I had to beat up and gang members who once jumped me calling and writing to me, begging for answers to escape those walls, not realizing that I too was still confined by walls just the same. My own battles raged on, even as I tried to help them find their way to freedom. Each message was a reminder of the chains that still bound me—emotional scars, haunting memories, and a lingering fear that threatened to drag me back into the darkness I had fought so hard to escape. I wanted to be their beacon of hope, yet felt like an impostor, trapped in a paradox of strength and vulnerability, yearning for liberation just as desperately as they were.

Political figures wanted to abuse my story and essence for their gains. Because everyone wants to feel like they were a part of something good. Only, I didn't feel good at all. I felt alone and I had no idea how to not feel that way. When you do time and have experienced severe trauma in life like I had, it forces you to pay attention to people in a way the average person just isn't quite aware of. You learn to pay attention to body language over words. Because the truth is, most people are just dying to tell you about themselves without ever saying a word. I noticed things and I just couldn't rock with it. I don't know when I could no longer see myself but, I'm sure it happened far before this point. By the time I had realized how far gone I was, my car was spinning out of control on the highway, crashing to a dead stop on a rainy night in August and the fall continued.

Let me start by saying this: I hate politics. It's a game where the players wear masks, smiling in your face while imagining how to strangle you from behind. That's the vibe I always got from it, and I despised every bit of it. Sure, there are some genuine people in politics, those who actually care about justice and doing what's right. But let's be honest—most of them are nothing more than control freaks playing with power, indulging in childish antics. It's a twisted theater where the audience gets hurt while the actors laugh behind the curtains. The deceit runs deep, and every backroom deal feels like a dagger aimed at the heart of true democracy. The promises made often dissolve like smoke, leaving nothing but disappointment in their wake. Watching this charade unfold only fuels my conviction that too many seek personal gain rather than the greater good. It's a world where integrity is often sacrificed on the altar of ambition, and the few who dare to challenge the status quo are quickly silenced, relegated to the shadows of a system that seems determined to maintain its grip on power at any cost.

During my post-release, my name began to ring bells in circles both far and near. My presence was felt, and not just by those who supported me. When I would go to court to watch and support my peers, I noticed something strange: the number of officers would suddenly increase. It was as if my very presence threatened them, and they responded with intimidation tactics. Detectives who had been on my case would go out of their way to antagonize me, poking at old wounds, reminding me of the nightmare I had fought so hard to escape. There were even times when officers, in their petty malice, would shoot air pistols at me—pathetic attempts to provoke a reaction, to make me lash out and give them the excuse they desperately wanted. It was an unsettling reminder that, even in my newfound freedom, shadows of the past loomed large, as if I were a ghost haunting the very halls that once held me captive. The tension was almost blinding, and I could feel the weight of their disdain pressing down on me, a constant reminder of the battle I was still fighting, both externally and within myself.

I sat in rooms with the Chief of Police scolding him about his dangerous remarks claiming that people are coming from Houston to his small town to commit violent crimes. You would think people in power would understand the power of words. A statement like that only places a target on a community's backs. I, like many other young men and women from Houston, came to San Marcos Texas for an education. Not to commit violent crimes. In that same room SMPD Detective Dwayne Poeboy latched out at me for my mere presence in the room. He turned red in the face and became shaky and sweaty as he barked like a dog with its back against the wall. The hatred was mutual, only now they hate me alone. As a great friend of mine once said:

"You can hate me forever, congratulations"
– King Rvcks

One occasion stands out in my memory. I was court watching for my friend William Spinks' trial, sitting quietly, observing, when SMPD Detective Patrick Aubrey—an individual whose soul seems as dark as the void, if he even has one—decided to lash out at me in the halls as I stepped out to use the restroom.

"Hey, you remember me? What's my name, huh? What's my name? You don't remember my name, do you?"

His cyclothymic nature was enigmatic. His voice dripped with arrogance, a twisted pleasure in trying to make me uncomfortable. I looked him dead in the eyes and responded, "Yeah, you're asshole number one, and that's asshole number two," pointing at his smirking partner, Dwayne Poeboy.

Aubrey, of course, wasn't satisfied. He strutted into the courtroom like he owned the place, set to testify as an "expert witness"—a title that couldn't be more ironic considering the lies I knew were about to spill from his mouth– this same detective told my friends; "Cyrus is f***ed he's going away for a long time," as he terrorized them for information that didn't exist. He seemed to suffer from extreme police bias:

Dr. Kim Rossmo, a Texas State University professor and criminologist, is widely known for his work in geographic profiling and criminal investigation methodologies. His research highlights how police bias—both implicit and explicit—can significantly undermine the integrity of a case. One of the primary ways bias manifests is through **tunnel vision and confirmation bias**, where officers develop an early suspect and unconsciously focus on evidence that supports their theory while ignoring or dismissing conflicting information. This narrow-minded approach can lead to wrongful accusations and prevent authorities from considering alternative suspects.

Another major issue is the reliance on **investigative heuristics and cognitive biases**, which are mental shortcuts that can lead to errors in judgment. Stereotypes about race, socioeconomic status, or past criminal records can shape an officer's assumptions about a suspect's guilt, often leading to misinterpretations of behavioral cues, forensic evidence, or witness statements. In some cases, investigators may even pressure witnesses into confirming their assumptions, increasing the likelihood of false confessions or tainted testimony.

Beyond individual biases, **institutional and systemic factors** also play a role in flawed investigations. Law enforcement culture can reinforce biases, especially when officers rely on flawed investigative tactics that go unchallenged. When there is a lack of leadership, oversight, and accountability, these biases persist, making wrongful convictions more likely. As a result, flawed investigations not only ruin the lives of innocent individuals but also allow real perpetrators to remain free, continuing to commit crimes.

Dr. Rossmo's research emphasizes the importance of **data-driven, scientific approaches** in policing to minimize bias. He advocates for methods such as geographic profiling, evidence-based decision-making, and cognitive bias training for law enforcement. His findings reinforce the need for greater oversight and reforms in investigative practices, as well as a shift toward more objective, analytical approaches to solving crimes.

Before he took the stand to begin his charade, he made a spectacle of my presence, loudly proclaiming that he wouldn't take the stand if I remained in the room. And he did this in front of the jurors, no less. The audacity was so outrageous that the judge actually paused the entire trial to hold a hearing on whether I should be allowed to stay. A few days later, William Spinks was sentenced to 40 years in prison. To this day, I can't help but wonder how much that unnecessary drama and Aubrey's self-serving antics influenced the jury and destroyed any chance of a fair trial for Spinks. It haunts me, a painful reminder of how easily justice can be manipulated by egos and power trips. These detectives are truly a disgrace.

Then there was Assistant District Attorney Gregg Cox, yet another puppet of the system, who took it upon himself to confront me in the courthouse hallway. He stopped, locked eyes with me, and told me exactly how much of an asshole and a threat he believed I was. Without hesitation, I affirmed his belief, reminding him he was nothing more than a cowardly bitch—unprofessional, disgraceful, and pathetic considering his supposedly "esteemed" job title. But Cox wasn't finished. That same week, as my back was turned in open court, he assaulted me. Right there, in front of everyone. And why? Because my very existence, my audacity to challenge the corrupt system he thrived in, infuriated him. It was as if my refusal to bow down to his authority wounded his ego, and he couldn't stand it.

That same day, he assured Joshua Wright's grieving family that nothing would happen to the officer who had shot their shackled loved one in the back six times, following his boyish antics. The paradigm of justice in this system are truly perplexing. When I confronted District Attorney Kelly Higgins about the matter, he mocked me, saying, *"You didn't hear the story? ADA Cox was trying to enter the courtroom, and you intentionally blocked the doors, so he had to maneuver around you."* His words dripped with contempt, a clear message that they would go to any lengths to protect their own, even if it meant lying through their teeth. It disturbed me deeply to realize just how unjust the justice system is, how my mere existence and triumph against their system was a threat they couldn't tolerate. Even those who had no direct hand in my case were hostile towards me, determined to cast me as their monster, no matter how little sense it made.

But that's the reality of politics, and the criminal "justice" system, isn't it? It's a stage where the truth is twisted, where power is the ultimate prize, and where people like me are crushed underfoot simply because we refuse to play along. I was never going to be their victim or their suspect, and they hated me for it. They reveled in their control, dismissing my struggle as a mere inconvenience, a fly to be swatted away. But I wasn't about to back down. Each time they tried to silence me, it only fueled my resolve.

I became a thorn in their side, a reminder that not everyone would bend to their will. My voice, once drowned out by their cacophony, began to rise above the noise, resonating with others who felt the weight of oppression. I knew that standing firm against their machinations would not only be my battle but a silver lining for those still trapped in the shadows. I was ready to fight, to expose their hypocrisy, and to reclaim my narrative, no matter the cost, and I still am.

"You're black balled Cyrus, you weren't supposed to fight back, you were just supposed to be quite and let it happen"
– Arty

This is what law enforcement agents have told me in literal words. I should've just shut up and let it happen. This is my reality, but I'm nobody's scapegoat. I'm your favorite problem solver and I get shit done. You can hate me forever, Congratulations.

Chapter VII:

Amy Kamp

"Injustice anywhere is a threat to justice everywhere."

— **Martin Luther King Jr.**

I'll never forget the day Amy Kamp stepped into Hays County Jail to visit me. Visitations and mail calls often stand as the emotional pinnacles of incarceration—moments of fleeting joy or profound despair. The brief euphoria of reconnecting with loved ones or receiving letters from them could lift you to unimaginable heights. Conversely, the crushing disappointment of your name not being called for visitation or mail could drag you into the abyss of hopelessness.

> **For anyone out there reading this who has a loved one incarcerated, I pray and urge you to remain by their side, no matter the cost or the challenges. Answer their calls, write them letters, and if it's within your power, visit them—visit them often. These acts, small as they may seem, can mean the world to someone facing such harsh realities. Your support, your presence, and your words can transcend the walls that separate you and help ease the deep isolation they feel. Remember, the strength you offer from the outside can be the very lifeline they need to hold on. Together we will always more.**

My mother, a beacon of unwavering support, made the long drive from Houston to San Marcos, Texas, whenever she could. Despite a harrowing car accident on her first visit, she never wavered in her commitment to comfort me during those short, 20-minute glass-shielded encounters. The day she brought my twin niece and nephew to see me was one of profound contrasts—one of the happiest yet most heartbreaking moments of my life. The last time I'd seen them, they were toddlers who couldn't yet speak. Now, they were chatting animatedly, full of questions about my absence and eager for my return. Their innocent joy soon turned to anguish as they realized my predicament. "What are you doing here? You're not a bad person," my niece said, her eyes reflecting a mix of sorrow and fierce support. My nephew added, "Yeah, you should break the glass and come home with us," his whisper tinged with hope and desperation.

I struggled to hold back my tears as I told them I couldn't. Their promises to return and their reassurances, "Don't worry, Uncle Baby-C. We're not gonna leave you here. We'll come back for you," only deepened my self-reproach for putting them in such a position.

As the guard arrived to end our brief 20 minutes together, I could only imagine the heartbreak and confusion they carried during their long drive back home.

When Amy visited me, I anticipated familiar faces but was instead greeted by a soft-spoken woman wearing a COVID mask. She introduced herself with kindness, explaining her purpose and intentions. She wanted to understand my situation and see who I truly was. Our conversation ignited a renewed determination within me.

From that day forward, Amy became an indefatigable advocate for my cause, even as she navigated her own pregnancy. She reached out to her media connections, fielded countless phone calls, and began advocating for me publicly. Her efforts included writing articles about my plight, relentlessly pursuing my lawyer to ensure he fulfilled his duties, and sharing my story widely. She attended every court appearance, documenting every detail meticulously, despite the challenges of bringing a new life into the world amidst the injustice she was witnessing. Amy's unwavering commitment and tireless advocacy for truth and justice not only bolstered my fight for freedom but also provided invaluable support to my family, fortifying our collective resolve.

Chapter VIII:

Professor Mathew Clair

"The only thing necessary for the triumph of evil is for good men to do nothing."—
Edmund Burke

Professor Mathew Clair of Stanford University emerged as a pivotal figure in my relentless battle for justice. I vividly recall the months leading up to my discovery of him—an era marked by my unyielding advocacy for myself and my fellow sufferers. I spent countless hours penning hundreds of letters to actors, advocacy groups, and celebrities, desperately seeking recognition of my plight, only to be met with silence. My days were filled with the monotonous hum of life behind bars, accompanied by the mandatory viewing of TMZ and sports, which provided fleeting distractions from the harsh reality we faced.

It was on one such day, amidst the monotony, that Professor Clair's voice cut through the noise. As he spoke about his book **"Privilege and Punishment"** on TMZ, my attention was immediately seized. The book, he explained, delves into how social privilege profoundly shapes experiences within the criminal justice system. Clair meticulously examines how class, race, and socioeconomic status influence interactions with justice and punishment, exposing entrenched inequalities that deeply impact those entangled in legal battles.

Listening to Clair, my mind raced with a desperate yearning to read his book. I felt an urgent need for the insights it promised, believing it held the key to transcending my dire circumstances. After the episode, I tracked down his contact information and, in a leap of blind faith, wrote to him. I shared my story and expressed how his work resonated with my plight, pleading for guidance on how to obtain a copy of his book.

The world, however, came to a standstill with the onset of COVID-19, and it took nearly two years to receive a response. When Professor Clair finally replied, his letter was a beacon of hope. He expressed how my letter had moved him, evoking memories of his own law school days. Clair's commitment to aiding me was unwavering. He answered every call, supported me financially, and attempted to send me a copy of his book—though it was sadly returned by the jail. He even collaborated with me on an article titled **Pretrial Injustice**, published in **Inquest**, a Harvard Forum.

Professor Clair's support extended beyond mere correspondence. He became a steadfast ally, a friend, and a true brother. His encouragement and unwavering support have been instrumental in my journey. To this day, he remains a pillar of strength and a source of inspiration, embodying the essence of genuine friendship and dedication.

Chapter IX:

Forgiven

"Forgiveness is the final form of LOVE"

- Reinhold Niebuhr

Chapter X:

As a Man Thinketh

"**I Killed A Man**" symbolizes the death of limitation—the breaking free from constraints, whether self-imposed or enforced by others. Each "man" represents a version of the self held back by fear, doubt, or societal pressures. By "killing" these aspects, we dismantle the barriers preventing us from reaching our full potential. Growth requires confronting and eliminating the limiting beliefs that keep us stagnant.

This chapter was originally meant to be a searing indictment of the state actors who dismantled my life—detectives, judges, police chiefs, sheriffs, and District Attorneys who wielded power with cruelty and indifference. I poured my rage into these pages, viewing them as embodiments of evil, existing solely to inflict suffering.

But as I revisited my words, I saw that they weren't driven by reason or righteousness but by raw, unfiltered pain. They were the cries of a wounded soul, lashing out in agony. The bitterness was palpable, every sentence a testament to the turmoil I was drowning in.

Time, however, has given me perspective. My feelings remain valid, but they don't have to mirror the darkness I condemn. I can acknowledge the injustice I endured without being consumed by it. My emotions, once chaotic, have been tempered by reflection and a deeper understanding of the human condition.

Yes, I still believe these individuals acted with malice and caused unnecessary suffering. And yes, I still harbor resentment. But I now choose to articulate my thoughts with control, recognizing the complexity of their actions and the flawed systems they operate within. I'd rather be a silver lining than a dark cloud, though it's disheartening how many still believe in them. My words are no longer reckless flails of trauma but measured reflections from a man who has faced darkness and emerged with understanding.

During my incarceration, my father sent me *As a Man Thinketh* by James Allen. The book explores the power of thought in shaping character, circumstances, and destiny. Allen emphasizes that by cultivating positive, disciplined thinking, individuals can transform their lives. One line stayed with me:

"A man is literally what he thinks, his character being the complete sum of all his thoughts."

After my release, my mind was trapped in rage and uncertainty, weighed down by trauma and triggers I barely recognized. I hid my struggles, drowning myself in work and distractions until I collapsed under the weight of it all. I accumulated financial debt, faced arrests in multiple counties for trivial things, lost my best friend through my own foolishness, and broke more hearts than I can count. I wasn't sleeping, lost over fifty pounds, and needed to be force-fed because I refused to eat. My friends had to force me to rest—I was constantly running from something I couldn't escape. I was killing myself all over again, and they saw it even when I couldn't.

I fought desperately to get ahead—so far ahead that if the State of Texas ever tried to take my life again, they would regret it. Those were my thoughts – "they got my ***** up–"but those thoughts weren't born of the man I truly am. I was spinning in circles, finding peace only in the presence of my Twin Flame. She gave me reason to think intentionally again, creating space for me to be vulnerable and feel safe. But when I was away from her, I slipped back into the very skin I was desperate to shed. That's what the State of Texas did to my mind, my existence. It made me unhinged and I blindly accepted it rather than seeking help and overcoming it.

Thankfully, that man was short-lived, though he left destruction in his wake. These days, I think more clearly again.

Chapter XI:

I Killed a Man

"You may encounter many defeats, but you must not be defeated. In fact, it may be necessary to encounter the defeats, so you can know who you are, what you can rise from, how you can still come out of it."
— **Maya Angelou**

My Ongoing Journey of Personal Growth and Self-Improvement

From my perspective, the metaphor of "killing a man" represents the painful yet necessary process of personal evolution. Each "man" symbolizes outdated or harmful versions of myself that held back growth. To feel like myself again, I believed I needed to shed those layers—confronting, dismantling, and ultimately eradicating the parts of myself that no longer served me. It is not an act of violence but a conscious decision to embrace transformation and allow healthier identities to emerge.

"I Killed A Man" signifies reclaiming personal power from negative influences or toxic relationships. Each "man" represents a person, belief, or situation that stifled my true essence. To move forward, I had to confront and eliminate these influences, effectively "killing" their power over me. This reclamation empowers me to live authentically and take charge of my destiny.

Additionally, this metaphor reflects the end of self-sabotage, where each "man" represents self-destructive thoughts, habits, or behaviors that undermine my growth. By "killing" these detrimental aspects, I actively dismantle the barriers I created for myself, breaking cycles of self-doubt and insecurity. In the aftermath of my seemingly insurmountable misfortune, this transformation fosters resilience and enables me to embrace opportunities rather than fear them.

It embodies the idea of embracing change despite discomfort. Each "man" represents familiar yet limiting aspects of myself that I clung to out of fear or complacency. To evolve, I had to be willing to let go. This metaphor encourages me to view change as necessary, not something to resist.

Finally, this metaphor speaks to my efforts to break free from the past and its hold on my present. Each "man" symbolizes memories, regrets, or failures that haunted me, preventing forward movement. By "killing" these remnants, I liberate myself from their weight, paving the way for a brighter, unencumbered future.

"There is nothing better than adversity. Every defeat, every heartbreak, every loss contains its own seed, its own lesson on how to improve your performance next time." — **Malcolm X**

In the depths of my struggles, I realized that to grow and heal, I had to kill not one, but many men, multiple times. These "men" were not physical beings but reflections of unhealed, unwanted versions of myself. Each represented a part of me that had served its purpose but was no longer needed. Letting go wasn't easy—it required sacrifice, introspection, and the courage to confront my deepest fears. Yet, by doing so, I made space for my divine self to emerge, rooted in strength, resilience, and authenticity. This ongoing process has allowed me to reclaim who I truly am—unburdened by the past and open to the future.

The first man I had to kill emerged from the crucible of my wrongful incarceration. Years behind bars filled me with rage and resentment, emotions that threatened to consume me. The fiercest battle was not against external forces but against the man I was becoming—one increasingly consumed by anger and despair. In the silence of my confinement, I made a crucial decision: to eradicate that version of myself. Letting go of the fury that had taken root in my soul was not easy. The struggle was brutal and relentless, but despite setbacks, I emerged victorious, paving the way for peace and resilience.

Another man I had to kill was shaped by poverty and the harsh realities of being a Black man in America. He carried the weight of hopelessness and defeat, molded by police abuse and systemic oppression. To rise above these challenges, I had to shed this identity—to kill the part of me that accepted these limitations. The victim mindset had to go. The procrastinator had to cease to exist. The stereotypes had to be obliterated. I chose to embrace my worth and purpose, dedicating myself to growth and healing. This man almost ended my life more times than I can count.

The man I am currently fighting is perhaps the most insidious adversary of all. He has reemerged in a more malevolent guise, forged from my struggle to escape wrongful incarceration. Born from the chaos of reentry and unaddressed PTSD, he haunts my every move. This version of me channels turmoil through reckless behaviors: manic spending, vices, fleeting relationships, and an obsessive drive for productivity as avoidance. He embodies a toxic mix of inherited dysfunction, narcissism, and unresolved trauma. Plagued by fear of failure and inflated pride, he has crafted an unhealthy god complex that borders on psychopathy.

The battle against him is not just about personal redemption but about reclaiming my identity. Confronting this man means dismantling walls of self-destruction and challenging demons that threaten my progress. This fight is relentless, often painful, but necessary.

This man has been terrorized by district attorneys, detectives, police, and broken relationships. He carries trauma—heartbreak, PTSD, dehumanization, and a constant fight for survival. He is shattered yet still fighting. This man is dying to live, and his existence would be the death of me. But despite the chaos he brings, I am winning the battles.

These men are not Cyrus Lua Gray III, if anything they're Cyrus-the-Virus a collection of layers—life experiences, learned behaviors, generational influences, and mental scars. Each must be peeled back, examined, and discarded to uncover my true essence. The process is grueling but necessary for healing and growth. Cyrus-the-Virus isn't good for anyone, not even himself.

This journey of self-destruction and rebirth is not for the faint of heart. It demands facing my darkest parts, acknowledging pain and trauma, and making a conscious decision to let go. I am actively fighting and healing, shedding unwanted versions of myself to make way for a stronger, wiser, more compassionate Xyrus. This chapter is not just about battles fought but victories achieved. It is a testament to resilience, self-awareness, and the unwavering commitment to becoming my best self.

The journey requires dedication to healing my body, mind, and soul. It means confronting my past, acknowledging wounds inflicted by a broken system, and finding the strength to forgive—not just others, but myself.

Physically, I push my body to its limits, understanding that true strength comes from perseverance. Through fitness, I transform my physical being, shedding remnants of my former self.

Spiritually, I seek guidance and renewal, striving daily to rewire my mind. Some days, I fail more than I succeed, but I continue pushing forward, accepting my flaws as part of the process.

Emotionally, the process remains grueling. Anxiety, depression, PTSD, ADHD, self-doubt—all must be confronted. Each step forward requires killing the man defined by these struggles, embracing a future filled with hope and possibility. It is an ongoing pursuit of healing, a relentless commitment to growth.

I now understand the deaths of these men—each one representing a part of my past that had to die so I could truly live. My daily mindfulness helps free me from the chains of old identities, outdated beliefs, and generational habits that never served my growth.

Through this process, I'm allowing my best self to emerge. My dedication and sacrifices are not just for my own healing but to inspire others to confront their inner demons, shed limiting layers, and embark on their own journeys of self-discovery and transformation. This is my story—a testament to resilience, the power of change, and the courage to step into the light. You are not alone in your battles.

Chapter XII:

Looking Forward

"I am not afraid of storms, for I am learning how to sail my ship." —
Louisa May Alcott

This year marks a significant milestone—I turn 30. Since my release, I've grappled with the reality of lost time and missed opportunities. For so long, I existed in survival mode, but now, I embrace the fullness of my journey.

The number 30 carries rich symbolic significance, particularly in numerology, where it is tied to the concept of the circle, symbolizing infinity and completion. It is also connected to the cycle of time, as seen in a clock—essentially a circle divided into 12 sections—representing perfect balance within cosmic order.

Numerologically, 3 embodies communication, self-expression, expansion, and creativity, while 0 represents eternity, infinity, oneness, and wholeness. Together, 30 encapsulates creativity, communication, and spiritual awakening. It signals readiness for new opportunities, but it is ultimately up to each person to recognize and embrace them.

"The secret of success in life is for a man to be ready for his opportunity when it comes." — **Benjamin Disraeli**

In spiritual numerology, 30 often symbolizes higher consciousness, balance, and the transition from personal growth to a deeper understanding of one's purpose. It marks the end of a learning cycle and the beginning of new challenges, where wisdom and clarity guide the way forward.

Balance and harmony are also key aspects of 30, representing equilibrium between the physical and spiritual, the self and the collective. It resonates with creative energy and manifestation, encouraging individuals to harness their talents and align them with universal principles. Service to others is another important theme, reflecting the idea that personal growth leads to a greater responsibility to uplift others.

Across various traditions, 30 is a turning point. In the Torah, it marks the age of priestly service, symbolizing maturity and readiness for sacred responsibilities. Joseph stood before Pharaoh at 30, stepping into leadership after years of hardship. Likewise, King David began his reign at 30, reinforcing its association with strength and transition. Jewish mourning traditions also recognize 30 days as a complete cycle of grief and renewal.

In Christianity, 30 is deeply significant—Jesus began His ministry at this age, stepping into His divine role. The prophet Ezekiel also started his prophetic journey in his 30th year. In both traditions, this number represents the culmination of preparation and the readiness for a higher purpose.

In the Qur'an, the number 30 is significant in spiritual discipline and growth. The fasting period of Ramadan, lasting up to 30 days, fosters self-reflection and devotion. Prophet Musa (Moses) spent 30 nights on Mount Sinai in divine preparation, and the Qur'an itself is divided into 30 sections for structured recitation. These associations emphasize spiritual refinement, discipline, and transformation.

While not universally symbolic in African traditions, numbers often represent stages of life, wisdom, and milestones. In many cultures, turning 30 signifies maturity, accomplishment, and a deeper sense of responsibility within the community.

Turning 30 symbolizes completion and a new chapter of self-discovery. I may not have it all figured out, but I find solace in my purpose, relishing the deep self-awareness I cultivate daily.

Life, for me, now knows no bounds, despite the State of Texas's relentless attempts to bring me down. I am at peace with the outcomes that have come my way. Yes, I carry scars and harbor anger, however I'm learning to navigate and channel these emotions with purpose. My path involves constant renewal, both mentally and spiritually. I've embarked on the much-needed journey of therapy to address my severe PTSD, though I'm still searching for the right therapist—ideally a brown-skinned woman with long legs and a tattoo down her spine. I'm eager to see how this search unfolds.

Looking forward, I am passionate about the possibility of returning to school for a law degree and committed to my financial, spiritual, and mental growth. Physically, I feel accomplished, today's life is more about gratitude and focus. I cherish the early mornings, watching the sunrise, working out and finding peace in the routine of cleaning my living space—an act of therapy rather than necessity.

"We don't develop courage by being happy every day. We develop it by surviving difficult times and challenging adversity." – **Barbara De Angelis**

As I write this book, DeVonte Amerson still currently faces the same unresolved charges that hang over my head. The State of Texas aims to secure a conviction on him, hoping to use it against me as well. Their tactics are diabolical, but we remain resolute and unyielding. My greatest advantage throughout this ordeal was defying their expectations of ignorance and passivity. I thank The Most High for granting me strength and resilience.

DeVonte and I were accused of Capital Murder, a charge carrying life imprisonment without parole or the death penalty.

Our opponents underestimated our resolve to overcome their corruption, however I believe they understand our determination now.

This journey is far from over. I hope my story resonates with readers and inspires bold action against our flawed justice system. We seek justice, not mere convictions; we need support and resources, not increased policing. Our system, rather than protecting and serving, devastates, criminalizes the marginalized, and shamelessly ruins lives. Police violence, wrongful convictions by politicians and district attorneys, and the deliberate disregard for justice are unacceptable and an embarrassment to this country.

Justice for Joshua Wright is Justice for Malachi Williams who was wrongfully gunned down by San Marcos Police department near the local HEB that thousands of students and citizens visit on a daily basis; Justice for Pam Watts and Jennifer Miller is Justice for Rodney Reed who still sits on death row today after wrongfully being convicted for the murder of Stacey Stites in the 90s; Justice for Bobby Harper who was wrongfully sentenced to life in prison at the young age of 17, over 20 years ago by the same prosecutor and forces in Hays County that vehemently attempted to force the same fate on DeVonte Amerson and myself is Justice for all who suffer under a system that works against the American people.

So when you see me or think of me, know that, YES, I did kill a man, but it wasn't the one I was accused of in cold-blooded murder. It was the man who settled for anything less than true freedom, prosperity, and altruistic service to others. Embrace love, spread peace, but above all, be relentless in your pursuit of truth, righteousness and justice, no matter the cost.

"To be free is not merely to cast off one's chains, but to live in a way that respects and enhances the freedom of others."
— **Nelson Mandela**

Chapter XIII:

Lessons Learned

"Our greatest glory is not in never falling, but in rising every time we fall." –
Confuciusz

I learned many things over the years of my struggle and journey. These are just a small glimpse into the world of knowledge and understanding I dove into within myself, my experiences, and literature.

1. Resilience in the Face of Change

- Life often demands us to adapt to new environments and circumstances, but through resilience, we can find strength and growth even in the most challenging times.

2. The Power of Family

- The bonds of family are foundational, providing support, love, and a sense of belonging that can help us navigate the complexities of life.

3. Sacrifice and Responsibility

- The sacrifices made by those who love us, like a mother working multiple jobs, often go unnoticed but are pivotal in shaping our lives and character.

4. Cultural Diversity Enriches Us

- Embracing the rich tapestry of different cultures, as seen through the family's roots in various West African countries, teaches us the value of diversity and heritage.

5. Community is Vital

- A strong sense of community and belonging is crucial for emotional well-being, highlighting the importance of collective support and togetherness.

6. Strength in Adversity

- The challenges of poverty and frequent upheaval can either break us or build us; with the right mindset, they can forge unparalleled strength and resilience.

7. Love Transcends Material Wealth

- True love and care are not measured by material wealth but by the willingness to give whatever one can, even if it's a small gesture like buying a game console.

8. Adapting to New Cultures

- Moving to a new country brings cultural shock, but it also offers the opportunity to learn, grow, and find one's place in a larger, more diverse world.

9. Empathy and Understanding

- Growing up in a multicultural environment teaches empathy, helping us understand and relate to people from all walks of life.

10. The Importance of Childhood

- Childhood experiences, whether filled with joy or struggle, leave an indelible mark on our identities and play a significant role in shaping our future selves.

11. The Importance of Self-Advocacy

- In situations where the system fails, it becomes crucial to advocate for oneself and for others who cannot speak up.

12. The Cruelty of Injustice

- The justice system can be deeply flawed and dehumanizing, often treating people as guilty until proven innocent.

13. Endurance Through Mental Anguish

- The mental and emotional toll of incarceration can be more damaging than the physical experience, requiring immense inner strength to survive.

14. Rebuilding After Trauma

- The process of rebuilding oneself after trauma is long and difficult, but it is essential for moving forward.

15. Hope Amid Despair

- Even in the darkest moments, hope can be found. Whether it's through the arrival of a new ally or the belief that justice will eventually prevail, maintaining hope is vital to continuing the fight.

16. Trusting the Right People

- It's crucial to discern who is genuinely on your side. While some may seem supportive, their actions may tell a different story. Surround yourself with those who truly understand and support your fight.

17. The Value of Small Victories

- In oppressive environments, finding and celebrating small victories can provide the strength needed to keep going.

18. The Pain of Lost Time

- Time lost due to injustice is a painful reality, but it can fuel a determination to make the most of the time that remains.

19. Transformation Through Suffering

- Suffering can lead to profound personal transformation, revealing aspects of oneself that might never have been discovered otherwise.

20. The Unbreakable Human Spirit

- Despite efforts to break the human spirit, there is a core of resilience and defiance that can never be fully extinguished.

21. Self-Transformation Requires Sacrifice

- To become the person you're meant to be, you must be willing to let go of past versions of yourself that no longer serve your growth. This process can be painful but is essential for true evolution.

22. Embrace the Journey of Self-Discovery

- Personal growth is an ongoing journey that involves confronting your deepest fears, traumas, and weaknesses. It's about peeling back the layers of your identity to uncover your true self.

23. Healing is a Holistic Process

- Personal transformation involves the mind, body, and spirit. True healing requires addressing all aspects of yourself—physical fitness, mental health, and spiritual well-being.

24. Victory Over Self is the Greatest Triumph

- The most significant battles are the ones fought within. Overcoming the darker parts of yourself is a victory that leads to a more fulfilled and purposeful life.

Special Thanks

"A person is a person because of other people"
– Ubuntu Proverb

This book would not have been possible without the generosity of those who supported, encouraged, and believed in its purpose. Your kindness and contributions made its publication a reality, and for that, I am eternally grateful. This is my special dedication to you—the individuals whose generosity helped bring this work to life. Just as you have been a part of my healing, you are now forever woven into the fabric of this manuscript.

MANO AMIGA

Shannon FitzPatrick

Merald S. White

Kecia Lewis

Bobby J Harper

Sherri Goodman

Cyrus L. Gray Jr.

Germod Williams

Alice N. Gray

Seth Mckenney

Dana Johnson

Anthony Betta

Riley Apel

J Gotfredson

Karen M. & Ricky T

VRW Merchandising LLC

Shawn Jackson

Myles Martin

NMB Solutions LLC

Amy Kamp

Pro. Matthew Clair

Ron B.

Rebecca Webber

Pastor Darius Todd

Janet Gockerman

Carnillius Green

Demun Mercer

Asad Asad

Charlie Sears

Mary Kahle

Soledad Prillaman

Lauren Oertal

Edwin Esquivel

New Money Business LLC

Anonymous Donor

Anonymous Donor

Anonymous Donor

A Letter To Attorneys

PTSD: Put The Stigma Down
By Xyrus

My name is Cyrus Gray, and for five years, I lived a nightmare—wrongfully incarcerated in Hays County Jail in San Marcos, Texas, falsely accused of capital murder. My brother, DeVonte J. Amerson, endured the same injustice for six years, and he is still fighting through a harsh and sorrowful system to this day. Incarceration is more than just physical confinement—it is a slow suffocation, a relentless psychological assault that breaks the spirit as much as the body. The weight of injustice sat heavily on my shoulders, pressing down with every passing minute, every endless day. But what made this burden unbearable wasn't just the bars that confined me—it was the attorneys who were supposed to fight for me yet left me feeling more abandoned than the system that imprisoned me.

Throughout my incarceration, I cycled through four attorneys—three during pretrial and two through trial. Not once did I feel secure or in good hands. These were individuals who had taken an oath to zealously represent and advocate for my defense, yet they did neither. Instead, they embodied the failures of a system that too often prioritizes expediency over justice, leaving defendants like me to navigate a legal maze with no guide, no voice, and no real chance at fairness. I had to become my own advocate, spending seven years actively fighting for my own freedom and for others caught in the same broken system.

The Tragedy of Bobby J. Harper

Bobby J. Harper's case is a gut-wrenching testament to what happens when a defendant is stigmatized, dehumanized, and abandoned by those meant to defend them. He was just a teenager when the system swallowed him whole—wrongfully convicted of murder in Hays County. The same system that tried to take my life. Instead of fighting for his client's life, Bobby's own attorney became another prosecutor in disguise, actively working against his best interests. His voice—along with the voices of his loved ones—was silenced, dismissed, and ultimately erased from the courtroom. The end result? Another young Black man condemned to a life behind bars, his freedom stolen before he ever had a chance to truly live.

Today, Bobby is in his 40s, still locked away, still fighting for the truth to be heard, still waiting for the justice he was never afforded. Decades have passed, and yet, the weight of that wrongful conviction has never lifted. He was left for dead by a system that never saw him as human—a system that didn't just fail him but actively worked to bury him. His attorney was the beginning of his unfortunate end. He refused to acknowledge Bobby's alibi, ignored witness statements that could have cleared his name, and shut out the pleas of his family. There was no zealous advocacy. There was no defense at all.

Bobby deserved better. At the very least, he deserved a fighting chance. Instead, he became another casualty of a legal system that discards people like him without a second thought. Another casualty of bad counsel. But we refuse to let his story end here. From the outside, we continue to fight for his long-overdue freedom, demanding that his name be cleared and his voice finally heard. Lawyers, you are the beginning. You hold the power to change lives—for better or for worse.

The Importance of Client-Centered Advocacy

Client-centered advocacy is the foundation of a fair and just legal system. It prioritizes the needs, rights, and experiences of the individual facing charges rather than treating them as a case number. Too often, public defenders and court-appointed attorneys operate under immense caseloads, leading to a disconnect between lawyer and client. However, true advocacy requires more than legal knowledge—it demands empathy, communication, and dedication.

When attorneys fail to engage with their clients, they strip them of their voice in their own defense. A defendant should be informed about their case, understand their legal options, and feel empowered to participate in their defense strategy. Effective advocacy recognizes that each client has a unique story, one that can often mean the difference between a conviction and an acquittal.

I often reference African Proverbs when I write because, well, they just make sense.

African wisdom teaches us, *"The one who asks questions does not get lost."* – Swahili Proverb. This means that communication is key—not just from attorney to client, but from client to attorney. When lawyers fail to ask the right questions, listen to concerns, or explain legal processes, they abandon their duty to protect the rights of the accused.

Going through my process, I asked, begged, and pleaded for my lawyer to do what I believed to be within his rights, duties, and capabilities. He would vehemently argue against it, just to tell me months later that it might have worked. The disconnect was infuriating.

Client-centered advocacy is not just about winning cases—it's about restoring dignity, ensuring fairness, and reducing the long-term trauma that incarceration can cause. Without this approach, the legal system will continue to fail those it was designed to protect.

The Impact of Attorney-Client Communication Failure

The Sixth Amendment guarantees the right to effective legal counsel, but what does that mean when attorneys don't communicate, don't advocate, and don't even seem to care? I spent years sitting in a cell with no updates, no explanations, and no strategy shared with me. The few times I did hear from my attorneys, I was met with indifference, misdirection, and a sense that I was just another case file—another statistic in a broken system.

My first attorney literally looked me in the face and said, *"Well Cyrus, you're guilty."* He then followed up by adding, *"I'll tell you what, I haven't looked into your case yet but if the judge makes me stay on it, maybe I'll see what I can do."*

This man visited me a total of five times in the two years he was my court-appointed attorney, and with each visit, I gained no better understanding of my defense nor the accusations and alleged evidence against me.

For many defendants, especially those wrongfully accused, this lack of communication leads to profound psychological distress. Imagine knowing your life's on the line, yet feeling invisible to the very person who holds your fate in their hands. The mental toll is immeasurable, and for some, it creates a lasting form of PTSD—Post-Traumatic Stress Disorder.

PTSD: The Invisible Sentence

Incarceration does not end at release. The trauma lingers, shaping the way we navigate the world. The distrust, anxiety, and emotional scars remain long after the cell doors open. But society often fails to recognize this. People assume that once we're free, we're healed—but freedom does not erase trauma. And the legal system, which should be a pillar of justice, often deepens these wounds instead of addressing them.

Attorneys, particularly those representing indigent defendants, must understand that their role is more than legal representation—it is human advocacy. Every defendant deserves to feel heard, informed, and involved in their defense. Without this, the legal system continues to be an assembly line of injustice, further traumatizing those it claims to protect.

The Path Forward: A Call to Action

For attorneys, my message is simple:

- Understand that your clients are more than names on paper. Their lives, their freedom, their families, and their futures depend on your commitment to ethical and effective representation.
- Clients should never feel left in the dark about their own cases.
- Recognize the trauma that defendants endure and treat them with dignity.

For the broader community, it is time to **Put The Stigma Down.** We must stop assuming that those entangled in the justice system deserve their fate. We must advocate for fair legal representation, systemic reform, and support for those who have suffered injustice.

I spent years of my young adult life in a hellish situation because I was stigmatized by a system and undervalued by my appointed attorneys. By my own legal representation. That's not okay, and that's not what fair defense, justice, or zealous representation looks like. I challenge you to **Put The Stigma Down.** Fair defense and Justice requires it.

Scan Me

بِسْمِ ٱللَّهِ ٱلرَّحْمَٰنِ ٱلرَّحِيمِ